*To my wife and family
and
to those sappers whose story
must remain untold . . .*

Acknowledgements

Information from the following sources is acknowledged and greatly appreciated:

David L. Smith (Ayr).

Donnie Nelson, Wigtown Free Press.

'The Longmoor Military Railway' by D. W. Ronald and R. J. Carter, published by David and Charles, Devon.

R. Wyatt, Longmoor Branch R.E. Association.

To my dear wife, Dorothy, my thanks for typing services.

Reproduction of cover painting—a Stanier Class 8F at work in the Middle East during World War II—is by George Heiron, commissioned by Chris Elliott.

Map on page 23 courtesy of 'Railway Magazine' from 'War Department Locomotives'.

The author would like to thank the following for permission to reproduce photographs in STEAM SAPPER:

H. N. James, Harry C. Deal, The Glasgow Herald, the National Maritime Museum, the Imperial War Museum, and the Central Reprographic Unit, British Railway Board.

It's years and years and years
            since I left my mother's knee
To go and be a Sapper
                In the Old R.E. . . .

Old war-time song . . .

Introduction

In 1940, Charles Meacher volunteered for war service with the Royal Engineers and was allocated the number 1940775 which was to become as familiar to him as the name he had lived with for 20 years. The relaxed routine of railway shift work gave way to Army discipline; the closeness of family and friends was displaced by the loneliness of a rookie in a strange environment—but not for long.

There is more to the Corps of Royal Engineers than marching and arms drill. These Army basics are complementary to the skills required in military engineering.

After training at Derby where a man-made smoke-screen foxed the Luftwaffe, the author was one of seven men sent to Cairnryan in his native Scotland as the nucleus of the 931 Port Construction and Repair Company, RE, their mission being to build a great military port. Here the reader can learn of the effort that went into this massive task.

From the relative peace of Wigtownshire the story moves to Eastbourne, the death-trap of the south in those days owing to the incessant hit-and-run German air attacks.

The author's military career then took him to the bleak moors of Hampshire and the Longmoor Military Railway, where over the years thousands of sappers trained to operate railways—and destroy them. Then his 'Home Guard' days came to an end and he was shipped to North Africa—thence to Italy—following the motto of the Royal Engineers—'Ubique'.

The significance of the saying 'Once a Sapper, always a Sapper' lies in the fact that the title transcends rank.

This book identifies with the common denominator that describes the versatility of the soldier-artificer.

Preface

The Corps of Royal Engineers (RE)

There were military engineers in Britain from Norman times but the corps did not receive its designation as Royal until 25th April 1787. With its sister regiment of the Royal Artillery it has the motto *Ubique; Quo fas et gloria ducunt.* In 1812 the School of Military Engineering was founded at Chatham. Charles Pasley, its first director, was a versatile genius to whom is owed Portland cement. The Royal Engineers, or as they are popularly known, the sappers, have had a hand in the development of practically every new military invention (famous examples were the Brennan torpedo and the Bailey bridge). Usually the fledgling has been nurtured in the corps until it is capable of flying by itself, when it is turned over to a specialist corps. Examples are ballooning, mechanical traction, telegraphs and camouflage.

Until 1st January 1947 the corps was organised in companies, each with a strength of 200 to 250, and with a number and a name giving an indication of its duties. Thus there was the Fortress company, the 5th Field company and so forth. From the above date it was organised in regiments, squadrons and troops, and was thus brought into line with other arms. New units such as depot regiment, corps engineer regiment, independent parachute squadron and movement control squadron came into being, a regiment being commanded by a lieutenant-colonel. The senior engineer officer of a corps is designated a commander corps (CCRE); an army has a chief engineer (CE) while larger formations such as army groups have usually had an engineer-in-chief (E-in-C). From 1804 to 1904 the senior engineer officer at headquarters in London was the inspector general of fortifications (IGF). Thereafter when the war office came into being he was known as the director of fortifications and works (DFW) until in 1941 an engineer-in-chief was appointed.

The engineers have always been responsible for the development of fortification and for the attack on the enemy land fortifications by means of sapping and mining: tunnelling, too, still plays an important part in warfare as a means of giving protection to personnel and stores. The

9

tunnel system of Gibraltar, constructed in the years 1940—45, is a case in point.

Throughout the Second World War bomb disposal companies of the RE worked unremittingly at the task of rendering harmless enemy bombs which had failed to detonate. Some figures which show the magnitude of the task are:-

Unexploded HE (high-explosive) bombs disposed of by RE:

In the United Kingdom, upwards of 45,000.
In NW Europe, upwards of 12,000.

The Bailey bridge, which was first used in the North African campaign 1942—43 was developed at the RE Experimental Bridging Establishment from the original idea of Sir Donald Bailey, at that time the chief designer there. A specialised activity which calls for mention is the ordnance survey which was formally established by the Duke of Richmond, master-general of the ordnance, in 1791.

Royal Engineers played a great part in the development of India. Sappers served on railways, public works, irrigation and forestry, and directed the survey of India. On the purely military side the corps was organised in companies of sappers and miners in which most of the officers were British and the other ranks Indian.

Before the Second World War the peace establishment of the corps was rather over 1000 officers and about 10,000 other ranks. Between 1939 and 1945 it expanded to about 400,000. The normal method of entry for regular officers is through the Royal Military Academy, Sandhurst.

Another side of the corps' work is transportation and movement control, the staff work for which is performed by a branch under the engineer-in-chief. This branch is responsible for the building and maintenance of railways and for constructing and operating ports in war. During the Second World War the famous Mulberry artificial harbour was assembled in Normandy by a special task force of RE transportation troops. Military postal services are among the corps' specialised duties.

The sappers play no mean part in bolstering the morale of British servicemen and women throughout the world. It has long been realised that regular receipt of letters from home is a great tonic for sagging spirits, therefore an efficient postal service for the Forces is important. The decision to enlist the talents of the sappers for this work has proved estimable and a brief history of the development of the Army Post Office warrants mention here.

As far back as 1799, a need for a Postal Service for the troops in the field was considered to be essential. It was not, however, until 1808 during the Peninsular War that the first Army Base Post Office was put into operation. Apart from this first Army Base Post Office and another in 1840, in the Chinese War, no proper postal service generally available for troops had ever been put into operation. On 22nd July 1882, Queen Victoria authorised the formation of the Post Office Corps which was formed from the 24th Battalion Middlesex Volunteers for service in the Egyptian and Sudanese campaigns. The Post Office Corps was then followed by a second Army Postal Corps called The Royal Engineers Telegraph Reserve. In 1889 both Reserve Corps were re-organised into two supplementary companies to give an efficient Postal and Telegraph Service during the South African War. 1908 saw a further re-organisation of the two reserve companies when they amalgamated into the Royal Engineers (Postal Section)—RE (PS).

The RE (PS) served during the First World War in France, Belgium, the Dardanelles, Egypt, Palestine, East Africa, Greece, Italy and North Russia. The ingenuity and resourcefulness of RE (PS) personnel was unlimited. As well as by conventional means mail was transported by mule, sleigh, trawler, mine sweeper, in fact any form of transport available at the time.

The Home Postal Depot was formed in 1914 to fulfil two functions. Firstly it served as a central sorting and distributing point for all forces mails, and secondly, for the training of RE (PS) personnel.

From 1918 until 1929 a nucleus of RE (PS) remained in the Army of the Rhine until it was withdrawn in 1929, whilst a detachment also operated in North Russia during the period 1918—1919.

During 1918 experiments were carried out using modified aircraft for transporting troops' mail by air. As the tests proved successful the first regular airmail service from Folkestone to Cologne was set up in March 1919 to provide the British troops in Germany with a fast mail service. This was the world's first scheduled airmail service. Due to the success of the Army airmail service, the system was adopted by civil Post Offices world wide.

The Second World War saw the RE (PS) serving on all fronts world wide and also detached with forward troops. During that war it was held by a famous Commander, that his troops could march for three or four days without food on the strength of one letter.

RE (PS) personnel landed with the Sixth Airborne Division by parachute and glider during the opening of the second front, and postal personnel were amongst the sea assault troops with the Fifth and Sixth Beach Brigades. Field Post Offices were established on the beach-head within hours of arrival.

Every day a special train left an LNER station in Nottingham with box wagons crammed to the full with a precious load, and raced through the night to a south-east port. The cargo? Six thousand mail bags filled with news from home. This was the daily post train to the British Liberation Army in Europe.

No matter where the letter or parcel was posted in Britain, it was first sent to the huge Army Post Office in the Midlands. Sorting of this tremendous mail was done by ATS girls and sappers of the Royal Engineers. The filled mail bags, directed to individual units in Europe, left in a continuous stream to be loaded 300 to a wagon, on a special train. Each bag contained an average of 95 news packets and nine parcels.

No train was nursed more than this. No train was regarded with more affection by those whose duty it was to safeguard this eagerly awaited mail from home. Though railway officials prompted signalmen that delays to the train had to be avoided at all costs, such reminders were not needed. In fact, the train often threw schedules out by being much before time and on one occasion was actually half an hour too early. This magnificent effort was carried on by the sappers in the field and just as the mail was delivered on the beaches at Dunkirk so, too, did the Corps of Royal Engineers complete the link between home and battlefront when our Army was on the offensive.

With the inclusion of British troops as part of the United Nations Forces in the Korean War in 1950, RE (PS) played its part in the support role to two Brtitish Brigades and with a line of Communications Unit in Japan.

In the early fifties the formation of NATO, SHAPE, HQ AQLFCE and HQ AAFCE saw the reintroduction of Postal units in France. The withdrawal of British troops from Egypt meant the transfer of the Middle East Command to Cyprus and the establishment of units in Aden and Tripoli. It soon became apparent that the RE (PS) provided a higher standard of service than that of their civilian counterparts with the consequent demand from Commands for BFPOS to serve in all overseas Commands.

An experiment was tried in 1953 whereby the Army Postal Service undertook the responsibility for the transmission of classified mail in BAOR. By a gradual progress, the transmission of classified mails worldwide was transferred to the RE (PS), a service which parallels itself in, but is separate from, the mail service.

Following the consolidation of the Service in the fifties the RE (PS), by now RE (Postal and Courier Communications), became organic to every field formation.

In 1962 the Home Postal Depot moved its location from Acton to its present location in Mill Hill and accepted the responsibility of the HM Ships mail from the civil post office, thus the RE (PCC) became a Tri-Service organisation, (having previously accepted responsibility for RAF mails) and an international military service with its units in NATO.

1974 brought the rationalisation of the UK Forces Courier Services and the introduction of Courier Wing within the Home PCC Depot RE. This Wing accepted the transmission of all classified document carriage within UK in addition to the existing worldwide service.

Further re-organisation took place in 1979 to form the Forces Postal and Courier Service into four PC Regiments and the Depot at Mill Hill renamed Postal and Courier Depot RE.

Today RE (PS) personnel will be found serving in UK, including Northern Ireland, Canada, Belize, Kenya, Brunei, Hong Kong, Korea, Thailand, Nepal, Cyprus, Italy, Sardinia, Gibraltar, Portugal, Germany, Belgium, Holland and Norway, all with the express intention of providing a service par excellence to the members of the three Armed Services.

During the past century the two greatest figures produced by the corps have been Gordon and Kitchener. Other important figures include Pasley, Burgoyne, who held the post of inspector-general of fortifications from 1845 to 1868, and Reid, a colonel of the RE, who was the adviser to the prince consort as regards the Great Exhibition of 1851.

The Institution of Royal Engineers to which nearly all regular officers of the corps belong publishes the Royal Engineers Journal and professional papers. The Sapper is the journal of the rank and file. The RE band is one of the most famous military bands in the army, and the regimental march is 'Wings'.

The head of the corps is styled the chief royal engineer, and the Queen in colonel-in-chief.

As can be seen the corps was steeped in tradition long before I joined the ranks. I was perceptive to the handing down of opinions, practices, customs etc., and I soon realised the pride in belonging to this body of troops. With such an illustrious background one was aware of a true sense of dignity. Other regiments also had traditions to live up to but mostly they were concerned with battle honours. Being 'first in the field and last to leave' the Royal Engineers rightly claimed the motto *Ubique*, but the corps was also unique. Apart from its fighting prowess the sappers had contributed a great deal to civil and military engineering. The activities detailed in the foregoing brief history indicate the wide range of tasks carried out by the soldier-tradesmen and they seem infinite. During my time in the RE's, I adapted to a variety of jobs, met a lot of people, and visited many places. In the following pages you can read about some of these activities.

Chapter One

When Britain declared war on Germany on 3rd September 1939, I was a discontented 19 year old working as a locomotive fireman on the London and North Eastern Railway. Most young people are dissatisfied with life during their formative years, and life as I knew it in Edinburgh was the dull routine of shift work on the railway with some light relief at the cinema, or dancing on a Saturday evening, providing I was on a suitable shift. My idea of something to look forward to was finishing work off the back shift in time to hear late night dance music on the wireless. Sunday was the worst time, when places of entertainment were closed and relaxation came in the form of a walk along Princes Street, a visit to the speakers corner at the Mound, and a fish supper on the way home.

When the phoney war culminated with the British Army's retreat from Dunkirk I was stoking a pug fire at Leith Docks. The occasional air raid and the arrival of the destroyer *Cossack* with released seamen prisoners from the notorious *Altmark* were incidents which confirmed there was a war on and of course there were blackouts, gas masks and rationing to remind us life had changed somewhat.

But for me it had not changed enough and I yearned for the atmosphere of adventure, the romance we associate with war and chivalry, a life different from the humdrum routine of work, eat, and sleep.

Along with my good friend Tom Campbell, I had already registered for military service with the '20' age group. We had both been medically examined and passed A1. But, being railway workers we were in a reserved occupation and could not be accepted in the Forces. A recruiting officer suggested we should apply to the railway company for our release and acting on this advice we wrote letters and handed them in at our depot office.

Tom fancied being a sailor and I was soon attracted to this visionary idea. Walking home after a night out we had something exciting to talk about and anticipate. We told our mates at work of our intention and they were gladdened by our spirit of adventure.

The initial excitement soon wore off and we were once again back in the old routine. Weeks went by and we had practically forgotten the mood of precipitating adventure when, out of the blue, we received letters saying we could be released for military service. It was something of an anticlimax to our alternating moods and we had lost the initial urge to go to war. However, we had committed ourselves to some extent by asking to be released from the railway and we had told our friends we were 'joining up'. There was nothing else for it but to present ourselves at the Music Hall in Edinburgh's George Street, the main recruiting centre, and 'face the music'.

The Senior Service had offices on the third floor and our hopes of a naval career were high as we admired wall coverings depicting a life on the ocean waves. When we enquired about our chances of climbing aboard we were amazed to learn recruiting for the navy had been suspended. The man we spoke to did not say why but it could well be the great influx of recuits had caused a bottleneck hold up somewhere.

Rather than be outdone we decided to try the RAF on the second floor. Here we were asked for all kinds of educational certificates but having had only a primary and secondary school upbringing a 'qualifying' pass meant little to the RAF. That was it then, there was nothing for it but to return to St. Margaret's depot and the railway.

As we were leaving the Music Hall we were attracted to a display of photographs showing railway troops in action. I knew such people existed because a few St. Margaret's men were on the 'Reserve' and went every year to Longmoor Camp in Hampshire to train. Looking at the photographs it seemed to us an attractive life and we turned about and presented ourselves at the Army desk on the ground floor.

The Recruiting Officer was delighted to see us and when he learned we were railway firemen volunteering for military service with the LNER's blessing he could hardly contain himself. As volunteers we had to take the Oath and although we had had a medical with our age group another physical fitness test (five doctors) was soon arranged and we were in the Army. It was 12th August—the start of the grouse shooting season. We were given certain documents and a travel warrant and told to report at Siddals Road Barracks, Derby—home of the Royal Engineers.

Unknown to us the son of a St. Margaret's engine driver was also going our way and it was a pleasant surprise to receive the lad's father at my home one evening. Driver George Henderson had heard of my impending departure to join the RE's at Derby and since his son Bob was embarking on the same journey, he thought it a good idea that Bob should go along with Tom and me. The more the merrier, I said, and so it was that Charlie, Tom and Bob found themselves on the 2150 (Army time) Edinburgh to St. Pancras train on 14th August 1940 en route Derby.

My parents had not been very happy about me going away but by the time we parted they had resigned themselves to my going. Dad was at the Waverley Station to see me off and Tom's dad was there, too. Both were aged about 42 and had seen active service in the first war. They had told us what fools we were to leave a safe job and a secure home for the uncertainty of war service, but I think they realised we were no different from them at the same age. My Dad said he was older than his 16 years when he volunteered in the 1914 war. Having said our goodbyes we were soon on our way and as the train blasted from the tunnel at St. Margaret's I caught a fleeting glimpse of my old work place, its bright lights dimmed by black smoke belching from rows of steam engines. It would be six years before I returned to this grimy, friendly depot.

Before settling down for a sleep on the crowded train the three new recruits talked for a while. Tom and I were old hands at being away from home, having been redundant at St. Margaret's in 1936 with the choice of being paid off or going to Carlisle. We opted for 'the home of the biscuit industry' and spent nearly a year in that Border town—a very happy year. In fact, the engine on our train was manned by Carlisle men, and when at about 0030 we stopped at the Citadel Station, we went along for a chat with our old friends and watched the change of engines.

Once under way again we settled down in the comforting warmth of the train and as I waited for sleep to overtake, I was alone with my thoughts and the clickety-clack of the carriage wheels speeding over the rails. This is when solicitude stirred my emotions and I felt a wee bit apprehensive regarding what I had let myself in for. But it was a brief interlude quickly overcome by sleep.

Railway stations were drab and well used in wartime and at their most dismal in the grey light of dawn. This was when I first saw Derby (Midlands) station and the depressing sight did nothing to uplift my flagging spirit. After a night curled up on a carriage seat my clothes were creased and I felt cold and hungry. The saving grace about travel in those days was the ever open catering houses for servicemen and Derby was no exception. It was not long, therefore, before we were sitting down to a hot meal in the canteen outside the station, a place we were soon to know well.

We walked through the damp morning air to Siddals Road Barracks, when few people were about. The barracks were similar to many such places throughout the country and really came into their own in wartime. The Derby barracks were in a built up area with a huge iron gate barring the main vehicle entrance and a guardhouse immediately inside. There was a sentry on duty, wearing an overcoat over his battle-dress and I am sure he recognised us for what we were, even before we spoke.

After introducing ourselves we were admitted through the large gates and as these banged closed behind us I seemed to experience the awful hopelessness of entering a prison and being locked up and I wanted to be

16

home again with my ain folk. This feeling soon left me as we made friends with those on guard duty, and before long we had been given the necessary implements and were in the breakfast queue.

Apart from the permanent staff there was an intake at that time of about 50 men and the first few days were taken up with documentation, medicals and uniform and equipment issue. The trio from Edinburgh were given consecutive numbers—mine was 1940775, Tom '776 and Bob '777.

The Army is a real melting pot and men from all walks of life with different natures, styles and beliefs are all brought together to be welded into one purposeful unit. This does not mean we had to forget our civilian pursuits, on the contrary, two lads at Siddals Road brought their motor bikes into the Army with them and I shared with the others many pillion rides.

For a long time I had been used to men sharing the same job in life with the same hopes and fears. In the Army I found myself literally amongst butchers, bakers and candlestick makers, every imaginable trade was represented and of characters there were plenty. Fothergill was, in my view, the typical English eccentric.

He was well spoken and obviously had received a good education. His shoulders were lopsided and he walked with a distinct gait. In the barrack room at night when we were all in bed Mr. F. used to throw open the window wide and utter loud a fervent prayer. He was fearless and when the drill instructor, demonstrating bayonet fighting, pushed the bayonet close to Fothergill's throat the brave man never flinched but stood stalk still with a rigid tremble. This awkward soldier later joined OCTU and became a serving officer abroad.

On receiving my uniform I could not get out quickly enough. The forage cap was difficult to wear and after more or less walking beside it and viewing myself in shop windows I followed the example of others and stuck my cap in my epaulet. But, one had to be watchful for military police who charged the unwary with being improperly dressed and I had no desire to start my army career on jankers.

The two weeks at Siddals Road seemed much longer and my first impression of the army was favourable. CSM Brown was a real gentleman and far removed from the sergeant major image. Looking back now I realise it was in his own interest to be friendly, since there was a collection for him prior to the departure of every intake of men. We had a farewell drink with him in a nearby pub and were entertained by an old worthy who blew bubbles with spittle and sang 'I'm For Ever Blowing Bubbles'.

From Siddalls Road we went to Castle Donington, not far from Derby. The site of the famous racetrack had been taken over for more urgent business and had been turned into a large military camp. The entrance

17

to the camp was about two miles from Donington village and somewhat remote compared with our previous quarters. There was a lodge at the gate and this was used as a guardroom. It was a training camp and hundreds of raw recruits were being put through their paces. We joined them and slept 18 to a bell tent-feet to the pole.

The bugler was in our tent and when he blew reveille in the morning he used to sit up in his bed, stick the bugle through the tent flap and then blow as hard as he could. The horrible sound reverberated within the tent, but there was no immediate movement and the bugler went back to sleep. Eventually we would get up one by one and wander off to the ablution benches for a wash and shave. Even when we were flooded after overnight rain and the water was lapping against our beds there was no stampede to evacuate the tent, we just carried on as usual. I remember one old soldier telling me I would suffer in later life becuase of the wetting, and I have often had cause to recall his words.

Military training was intensive at Donington and we had six weeks of it. Unknown to us some of our NCO's had joined the Army only a few weeks before. They had to be promoted quickly to receive the new intake.

There was not much time for recreation and the only occasion I saw Donington village was on a Sunday when Presbyterians marched the two miles to church. Other denominations were catered for in camp and non-believers were put on fatigues. The latter quickly got wise to the situation and joined the Church of Scotland. Not only were we going for a nice walk to Donington, we were each adopted by church members and invited to supper in the evening.

When we ventured out on a Saturday night we sang loudly as we walked back to camp. It was here I learned Army songs and more especially RE songs. There was no light to guide us on our way but we knew we were near our abode when we heard the loud cry, 'Halt!—Who goes there?' The singing would abruptly finish and in chorus we would shout, 'Friend!' 'Advance, friend and be recognised,' called the voice from the darkness, and one by one we would step forward and be looked at in torchlight.

My turn for guard duty came round more than once and it was a wearisome two hours standing there in darkness, in the middle of nowhere. When the time came for the songsters to stagger towards me I was more than ready for them, as I exercised the power many looked upon as a mere duty. With one mighty shout I was able to hush the most unruly and sobriety came to them as they realised I was armed with 'one up the spout'.

Such light-hearted bravado was quite harmless and it was some kind of relief after hanging about alone on a cold, dark night. Bravado, however, was the farthest thing from my mind when I went out on dawn patrol with another soldier, armed with an ancient American rifle and five rounds of ammunition. Being soon after Dunkirk a German invasion was expected and we were on the alert for parachutists. What we would have done had some landed is something I never contemplated.

There is more to military training than square bashing and bayonet fighting, soldiers have to take their turn on camp duties, or 'fatigues' as they say in the Army. When my turn came I was detailed to assist in the Naafi kitchen. This must have been my destiny and indirectly I was heading towards matrimony.

In the Naafi I met a cook who had just returned from leave and during our conversation he told me about two girls near his home who were interested in writing to lonely soldiers and perhaps sending parcels. He gave me their addresses and one I passed on to Tom while I took on the other one myself. After an exchange of letters we swapped photographs. My pen pal's picture arrived while I was sunning myself outside my tent during a dinner break and I was very impressed by her good looks, so much so that I passed the photograph to a near neighbour and said, 'I'm going to marry that girl.' It came about that at Easter, 1941, I met Dorothy, my pen pal, for the first time. She visited me in Derby and we later courted by letter and were married in Edinburgh on 26th December 1941. Tom never took to letter writing so his destiny was shaped elsewhere.

Although one has a wide circle of mates in the Army a close affinity usually involves two or three. In my case there was Tom and a bright spark called Bill Shorrocks. Bill could speak all kinds of English and Scots dialects and it was difficult to decide on his origin. He had been in the Territorial Army and was smart in appearance; he knew his drill and was worthy of his single chevron. His attitude to military matters, however, appeared careless and relaxed and he was always last out of bed in the morning.

This meant he was trailing behind while dressing and washing and attending for breakfast. In fact his lateness ensured he had every place to himself and this could earn him leftovers at the morning meal. The difficulty arose when it was time for parade and as our bugler alerted those who were ready to fall in Bill was always in a state of undress. This was unfortunate because being the smart lad military-wise he was the automatic choice as 'marker' and the company needed a 'marker' to fall in on. More often than not as we hurried on to the parade ground Bill would be lacing his boots or tying his gaiters and looking up from a stooping position he would wink and say to me, 'Do the necessary, Chas.'

Being smart enough to be a 'marker' after only four weeks in the Army certainly boosted my ego and since the proper formation on the parade

19

depended on the 'marker' I had to keep my wits about me. I wanted our 'A' Company to be foremost in drill order as well as alphabetical order.

CSM Hendry was small in stature but impeccably dressed and he always wore kid gloves. What he lacked physically was compensated for by his military bearing and pleasant personality and his commands were clear and precise. His position on the parade ground was a preliminary warning to the men standing in groups that a fall in was imminent, but first there had to be some kind of a guide, so that the ranks could dress properly. As the CSM braced himself the chattering soldiers were hushed by the call, 'Right! Marker!' This was the marker's cue to take up his position on the parade ground and all eyes were on his deliberate movements as he marched to the appointed place and smartly halted at attention. 'Markerrrr—Steady!' was the next command, quickly followed by 'Companee—On Parade!' the emphasis being on the first syllable of both commands.

Although we could not see the other Companies, similar orders were heard echoing across the grassy slopes of Donington Park, another day of square bashing and physical effort was about to begin.

Corporal Davies was our drill instructor and he was obsessed with precision drill, so much so that he had a long mirror in his tent which he stood in front of as he perfected rifle movements. He was a dedicated soldier and a very sad man when he was recalled to railway service at Crewe where he had been a fireman. Many would have gladly swapped places with him but the system did not work in favour of the individual and what was best for the war effort.

Lording it over the whole Training Battalion at Donington Park was RSM James Cosgrove, who I had known slightly at St. Margaret's as a fireman, but not at all as the boss at Donington. With his service uniform and Sam Brown belt on he looked very smart and he had quarters in Donington Hall where he had the services of a batman. With good pay and conditions in the Army he was reluctant to return to the railways when hostilities ceased but, somewhat belatedly, ill health forced him back into civvy street and he was fortunate enough to be re-installed as a driver at St. Margaret's. The Trade Union opposed a return to his former position in the links, but in the immediate post war years the Locomotive Superintendent in Edinburgh was an ex-RE and I suppose he influenced the situation in Cosgrove's favour. Anyway, the former RSM became an engine driver and I progressed to be his supervisor. But, meanwhile, Jim was top man at Donington and I only knew he was there, our paths crossed not at all. It was years later before we got round to swapping experiences.

Chapter Two

By the time our training was completed at Donington winter was not far off. I had enjoyed the six weeks in the open air with occasional jaunts to local pubs and more ambitious motor bike rides to Long Eaton on two occasions. But, now it was time to move on and feeling more like soldiers we went to civvy billets in Derby and took over the Baseball Ground—the home of Derby County Football Club.

Tom and I were billeted with Mrs. Ammet in Shaftsbury Avenue where she lived with her husband and daughter Ivy. We had a strict code of conduct to live up to but having been away from city life for so long we were eager to have fun.

Our first venture out was to a late night dance and the proceedings included a singing contest. Being in good vocal form I took my turn at the microphone and gave my rendering of 'When the Poppies Bloom Again', a sad song with a war flavour. Such songs were banned for broadcasting by the BBC since they were inappropriate for a nation bent on winning a war, but my audience lapped up the sentiment and I won first prize—a gent's leather wallet. I later sent it to my Dad as a present.

We were late in getting back to our lodgings that night and found Mrs. Ammet sitting waiting for us and the lecture began, 'The boys who were here before you didn't keep late hours and you're not going to start it,' she said. 'I'll report you to your Commanding Officer.' We smiled down at her sitting there beside the supper table, her short legs barely touching the floor. She was dark in appearance with skin like leather and struck me as being a proper litle madam. Just as well Tom and I were in good fettle otherwise a row might have followed. As it was I bent my head towards her and said something like, 'Give's a kiss, sweatheart, we are sorry if we offended you.'

Her head turned away as she avoided my advances but I could discern a fleeting smile crossing her face. She was human, after all, I thought, and followed up with, 'Next time, we'll take you with us to the dancing.' This seemed to break the ice and she rose and busied herself preparing supper. From then on our misdemeanour was forgotten and Mrs. Ammet looked after us like a mother. When we were on guard at the nearby

Baseball Ground she brought hot soup to us and when the air raid siren sounded at night she was calling for us to get up and go to the shelter, but we never did.

The air raid shelter in the garden was the domain of Mr. Ammet. He used to sit every evening listening to the wireless with his cap and scarf near at hand. The air raid sirens usually sounded about seven o'clock and Mr. A. was off like a shot to the shelter caring nothing for his wife and daughter or anyone else. I remember one evening having a walk in the garden with Ivy to visit her father in his hideout. There he was stretched out on a bunk reading a book by the light of a lantern. When Ivy put her head in the door he said, 'What are you doing here—you're not frightened!'

Derby was a prime target for German bombers because of the Rolls Royce presence there and the making of aero engines and other weapons of war. It was also a difficult target because of the town's position in a valley covered by a man made smoke screen.

The Royal Engineers were responsible for the smoke screen and a filthy job it was too! Every morning the sappers went round the streets positioning and replenishing drums of crude oil. These were placed at intervals along the pavements and with the approach of dusk the oil was made to burn in such a way that greasy black smoke rose and formed a cloud-like canopy over the town. It could be a distressing experience to pass through the blackout curtain and the door of a house and emerge into the smoke filled night. Anyone with a chest complaint was in real trouble. The idea seemed to be effective and usually the German bombers missed Derby and headed for a more open target.

We were responsible for dealing with new intakes of men at the Baseball Ground. We provided a guard for the premises, handed out kits, and protected the recruits as they drilled on the car park. The grandstand proved ideal for lecture sessions.

There was a gun pit at the car park with a Lewis machine gun installed and we took turns at manning this post. I was very often paired with Tommy Norman, a talented pianist who had played with top bands in America. Tommy was less interested than I was in fending off possible air attacks and was completely engrossed in writing and studying music. In the evenings we teamed up together and found regular work in Derby pubs with Tommy playing the piano and me singing. A popular venue was Tommy Crilley's pub just round the corner from Shaftsbury Avenue and the ex-footballer landlord was always pleased to see us, for we attracted many customers. Consequently, our credit was good and when the money was tight we were always sure of a welcome and a drink at 'Crilley's Tavern'.

The Royal Engineers is a work force rather than a fighting force with the ideal being a combination of the two. The time had come to be sorted out and learn a trade. Bob Henderson had already gone for trade training direct from Donington. So it was that Tom Campbell and I found ourselves attending the LMS College in London Road, which by this time had been commandeered by the Army. We were sent to a camp at Alveston and went from there to the College every day for training in the operation of military railways.

There were all kinds of tradesmen on that course, some never having worked on the railway. In the beginning we were told to submit details of our work experience in civvy street and, not surprisingly, my practical knowledge matched that of Tom Campbell—we were both steam locomotive firemen with the same period of railway service.

We were also told that at the end of three weeks theoretical instruction four men would be selected for practical training on stationary engines. Others would study for four weeks and go on to footplate work on the Military Railway. I naturally thought I was a certainty for footplate work, but I soon learned my trade grading was to be Stationary Engine Attendant. My protests to the Officer in Charge at the College were shrugged off and I found myself posted to Weston on Trent where a large Nissen hut camp served as accommodation for trainees and others working on the Melbourne Military Railway.

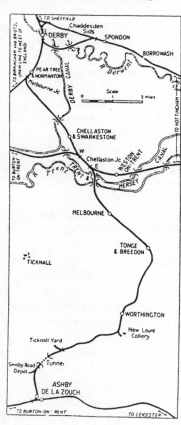

This stretch of line ran from Weston Quarry, where locomotives and other stock were stabled, to Worthington with Melbourne as an intermediate station where there was a small detachment of maintenance and operating personnel. The distance in all was 13 miles and the line had formerly been the Ashby de la Zouch branch of the Midland Railway.

At Weston, Kings Newton and Worthington there was a water supply for locomotives and at the Quarry this was drawn from the Trent and Mersey Canal by means of a Merryweather pump and stored in a large tank for use when required. The pumping equipment consisted of a single acting engine driving a pump and a small vertical boiler to supply steam for working the contraption. A large diameter flexible hose with strainer basket attached was the means by which the canal water reached the pump for delivery through another hose to the storage tank. The apparatus was completely portable and ideal for the purpose it served. It was on the Merryweather at Weston Quarry I started learning to be a Stationary Engine Attendant—and what a start!

I was detailed to take duty on the afternoon shift and learn from the man already on the job. The railway was not far from the camp and I walked to the pump site by the canal and duly reported to my instructor. He explained that the Merryweather boiler had been washed out that morning and consequently it was lifeless and without fire. My new colleague then went on to explain that he would have to go and look for wood to light the fire and forthwith departed from the scene. I was alone in the little house built into the canal bank and feeling strange in my new workplace, I sat down to await my friend's return.

Very soon I was engrossed in a paperback I had picked up and in the circumstances I could not do any more than await my instructor's return. I knew nothing about a Merryweather pump and had never seen one before in my life. As I sat reading I was aware of a shadow being cast over me and I glanced up to see two khaki clad legs descending the short flight of steps from the railway area above. Very soon two arms came in sight and on these were the unmistakable 'galloping horses' badges worn by an RSM. Still I did not budge, simply because everything was strange and I just did not know what to think or do. Then the man himself confronted me and I soon realised I had met up with a full blooded sergeant major. His face was crimson and his neck bulged as he raged and fumed at me. I did not quite understand what he was on about but he seemed angry about the pump being out of action.

Shortly afterwards a more friendly sergeant came to see me and asked for my name and number, etc., saying he had been given instructions to put me on a charge. There was a long queue of engines waiting for water and I was given the blame for not having the pump working. When the real culprit returned with some wood for the fire I told him about the furore during his absence, but he merely shrugged his shoulders and got on with the job of raising steam.

A few days later I was charged with neglect of duty and appeared before my OC, Captain Jenkins, who was nicknamed 'Wings' because of the RAF insignia he wore on his tunic. He must have been a qualified pilot before he came to the Royal Engineers or associated with aircraft within the corps. After reading out the charge he asked me if I had anything to say but it was obvious he was not prepared to listen so I did not say much.

'Alright, Meacher,' he said, 'two days CB.' This was quickly followed by a sergeant major's loud voice shouting, 'Right turn! Quick march! Left, right, left, right,' rapidly. Outside the office I was given my hat back and told to report for jankers on Saturday and Sunday, the two days I looked forward to most. It was at the weekend many of us made the nine mile bus trip to Derby but there was I washing dishes instead. I felt there was no justice.

My unfortunate initiation in my new job was soon forgotten and in no time at all I was in full charge of the Merryweather pump at Weston Quarry and keeping the storage tank well topped up. I also went to Worthington, where water was pumped from a stream, and although there was travelling involved, making a longer shift, I quite liked the rural setting and the peacefulness. There was an old inn not far distant across a field and here we could meet local farmers and enjoy fresh pub grub.

The trains were worked by former associates I had left behind at college and Tom Campbell and I were soon together again. We knew, however, it could not last long and we made the best of it. When we visited Derby we usually went to see Mrs. Ammet, but the outing would not have been worthwhile had we returned to Weston on the last bus at nine-thirty. If we went dancing it meant having to leave just as things were warming up. So, we usually walked back to Weston camp via Cuttles Bridge, a shorter route than that taken by the bus but still a very long walk. This route also had the advantage of taking us into camp by the back door, so to speak, and in this way we avoided the guard.

It was while I was at Weston that my pen pal, Dorothy, came to see me. As arranged I went to meet her off the train at Derby (Midland) station in the forenoon but she was not there. On returning to camp I had dinner then went with Tom to get a bus to Derby. As we waited with other soldiers at the terminus we saw the bus come in and passengers alight. One girl looked very like Dorothy, in fact, I was sure it was her, and I told Tom this. But instead of coming towards us and the camp she walked in the opposite direction and I quickly followed. I caught up with her on a little bridge well away from anyone else and I said, 'Who are you looking for?' 'You!' she replied and together we walked back to the bus and went on to Derby with Tom. I learned later she could not bring herself to face up to the crowd of soldiers and had deliberately walked in the opposite direction.

Bill Shorrock's landlady, Mrs. Yeomans, who had a house opposite the Baseball Ground, had agreed to put Dorothy up for the weekend and on reaching Derby we went at once to Mrs. Yeomans. It was an opportunity to get to know each other and my future wife saw for herself the places and the people I had written about in letters. The introductory photograph I had sent to her from Donington also included Tom and Bill

25

and I did not identify myself at first. Dorothy was faced with the problem of guessing who she was writing to. Now on her visit to Derby she was able to meet in person the three soldiers who had previously been photographic images. We all got on well together and had a very happy weekend, but all too soon Dorothy and I were parted for the first of many times after saying our goodbyes at the station. She returned to Haworth in Yorkshire and very sadly I went back to my Merryweather pump.

As if to remind us we were still in the Army we were on occasions subjected to exercises more in keeping with the infantry tactics. Someone in authority would suddenly decide we were growing soft on the job and our muscles had to be toned up. One of the most convenient ways of doing this was to send the men out on a route march and to add to the realism of soldiering they took their rifles and packs with them. It was on one such occasion I encountered another old acquaintance from St. Margaret's.

Like RSM Cosgrove at Donington, Sergeant Leslie Anderson had also been on the reserve when war broke out but there the similarity ended. While Cosgrove's rank reflected his military propensity and ability, Anderson had earned his stripes because of his Reserve activities and his trade qualifications, that is, his footplate experience. Leslie was no soldier and he sensed discipline rather than dispensed it.

About 30 of us stood idly in three untidy ranks, like schoolboys waiting to go into school, acting wildly like little boys and talking loudly. We were, in fact, anticipating the freedom of the open road and the carefree respite of a route march. Sergeant Anderson stood just as idly in front of the squad and when he thought we were becoming somewhat unruly he murmured, 'Steady now, lads, you don't know who's watching.' He eventually realised he was there to take us on a route march and again in low tones he said, 'Right, lads, left turn, quick march.' That was it, we moved off from camp like a shuffling crowd eager for admission to a football ground. There was no need for the sergeant to say, 'March at ease,' as is the usual practice on such an outing, we could not have been more at ease, or more slovenly.

I fully anticipated hours of marching along Derbyshire roads with occasional rest periods but we were no sooner out of camp when I was carried with the crowd into the 'Plough Inn' and there we remained, drinking beer and playing darts, until Leslie decided, 'It's time we were getting back now, lads.' We emerged from the 'Plough' in great form and straggled the short distance back to camp. Approaching the guard room a voluntary hush came over the 'marchers' and we suddenly appeared wearisome. Our tired state must have looked credible, according to the sympathetic looks we received from the guard.

Later, in 1947, when I was back in St. Margaret's, our job was off because of heavy snow on the Waverly Route and I sat with my driver Harry Campbell and many other elderly enginemen. These old timers got round to talking about lazy firemen and I smiled to myself when Harry said in his forthright manner, 'The laziest b----- I ever had for a fireman was Leslie Anderson. That b----- was too tired to put his head out of the cab and watch for signals.'

Leslie is too far away now to bother about such adverse criticism, but had he been able to hear Harry's comments I am sure his mild manner would have summoned forth only a pleasing smile. He was that kind of man, quite unsuited to the disciplines of war, or even work, but a very friendly person.

Weston camp is now a Ukrainian settlement and it is noteworthy in my case book as being the place where I faced my first charge in the Army. It was there, too, I experienced the Army's treatment, on a massive scale, for possible constipation. Their way of ensuring free bowel movement was to infuse the food with laxative substance resulting in the incredible scene of scores of men running from their quarters throughout the night and not making it in time for the latrines.

On the credit side, my work at Weston was a new experience to add to my bank of knowledge. NCO's were far from being 'charge happy' as I had at first thought. On the contrary, they were fun to work with and one sergeant, I remember, had an explosive sense of humour.

One morning at the end of a night shift men were sitting half asleep in the bothy at Weston Quarry. This jovial sergeant stood talking, with his back to the hot stove. Eventually he departed the scene saying something about it 'being time to get back to camp.' The drowsy night shift workers were in no hurry to leave the warm bothy and face the cold morning air and for fleeting seconds all was still after the sergeant's exit. Suddenly, there was one mighty explosion as the contents of the fire flew in all directions and wide awake men rushed outside. The sergeant was there laughing his head off, but he was called everything except 'sergeant' as the men realised he had deposited a railway detonator in the fire before taking his leave of them; not a very bright thing to do but amusing to some people.

I remember the rows of Nissen huts that made up the camp; the friendly banter among the occupants prior to bedding down for the night; the need to book an early breakfast if one was on early turn of duty; the friendly Wesleyan Chapel canteen in the village; but most of all I remember Weston-on-Trent as the place where I first met my wife, and it is because of this that our oldest son Brian has 'Weston' for a middle name.

Chapter Three

Having been well trained as a Stationary Engine Attendant I was now eligible for posting to a suitable Unit. I was pleasantly surprised, therefore, when I learned that my new abode was to be in Scotland at a place called Cairnryan, near Stranraer. I knew this to be the port serving the shortest sea route to Ireland, but that was all I knew about Stranraer and Galloway.

There were seven of us in the party that journeyed north, a lance corporal and six sappers. We were the nucleus of an entirely new company, the 931 Port Construction and Repair Company, and we were destined for the unknown in more ways than one.

Cairnryan was an unspoilt village in the early part of 1941 lying on the east shore of Loch Ryan some six and a half miles by road north of Stranraer. A most imposing structure is Lochryan House built in 1701 by the Agnew family on a very individual Dutch design and later inherited in the late eighteenth century by the son of Mrs. Dunlop of Dunlop. This man, one of Burns' correspondents, later changed his name to Wallace. There are Victorian additions to the house but it is largely unspoilt.

The Loch is an appendage of the Firth of Clyde and separates the northern part of the Rhins peninsular from the main land mass of Wigtownshire. Loch Ryan is about eight miles in length and has a maximum breadth of two and three-quarter miles. At its southern end, well sheltered from the wild winds of the North Channel, is the port of Stranraer.

The ship crossing from Stranraer to Larne has to travel eight miles in a northerly direction before it can head south-west for the Irish port. The southern part of Loch Ryan has no great depth of water and the dredged channel entails several changes of direction and a limiting of speed.

The Loch narrows to a breadth of one mile at Cairnryan where the houses are strung out along the main A77 road. While navigating the deep channel the 'Paddy Boat', as it is popularly known, comes near to Cairnryan lighthouse and nearby the lighthouse there was, in 1941, a bowling green and a clubhouse.

Our advance party pitched a tent on this bowling green and took over the clubroom for a company office.

When I stepped off the train at Stranraer I asked a porter how far it was to Edinburgh and he told me, about 130 miles. I had visions of a quick visit home before settling down in the back of beyond but I soon realised that it was easier to get from London to Edinburgh than from Cairnryan to Edinburgh. This reality became clearer as I sat looking out over Loch Ryan with the massive Galloway hills at my back; there seemed no escape.

During the early days of our sojourn on the banks of Loch Ryan we fended for ourselves and did our own cooking and washing. There were no parades and roll calls to bother about and our recreation was confined to long walks and some beachcombing. There was not a great deal of fraternising with the villagers who were unaware of the pending disruption to the peace of their rusticity. Their orderly life style and their oyster beds were soon to be torn asunder. One person, however, was due to reap a rich harvest, Mrs. Aitken, who ran the post office cum general store, the only shop in the village.

The influx of men commenced as a trickle and developed into a torrent. A large camp of Nissen huts was built on the heights above the village with a magnificent view over Loch Ryan. New intakes arrived every day and they came from many regiments. All had one thing in common, they had skills to contribute to the building of a great new port.

Before the outbreak of the Second World War, plans had been drawn up for two new ports for use in the case of Liverpool or Glasgow suffering crippling bomb damage. Military Port No. 1 was to be at Faslane, on the Gareloch, Port No. 2 was to be at Cairnryan.

The Cairnryan scheme was a formidable one, contemplating one and a half miles of wharfage, with a minimum depth at low tide of 33 feet. The plan was based on Cairn Point which projects some 400 yards into Loch Ryan. From Cairn Point massive wharfs parallel to the shore were to be built out to north and south for distances of 300 yards and 700 yards respectively. One mile to the south, another little promontory provided a base for a lighterage wharf 500 yards in length.

Sanction had already been given for the construction of the two ports in August 1940, the month I joined the Army. This being so, it seems I was fated to participate in the scheme, and the commencement of work was arranged to coincide with the completion of my training as a Stationary Engine Attendant. The task at Cairnryan was a very big one, involving a large amount of dredging. Equipment at the port was to be on a large scale with 31 wharf cranes, together with a 60 ton hammer head crane at the approach to the south deep water wharf.

As a 21 year old sapper I knew nothing of these statistics and the purpose of my being in such an isolated place. I soon realised, however, that soldiering was out and hard work was the order of the day, 24 hours a day.

We moved into the new camp above the village when it was tents and a mere two huts but there were soon many more and when they were given numbers I was in Hut 29. In the beginning there was no Naafi or recreation facilities. Stranraer was more than six miles away and boasted a single cinema and two canteens. In the other direction there was a journey of 30 miles to Girvan and the limited entertainment that town had to offer. We were on our own and Mrs. Aitken in her general store took full advantage of the situation. If a soldier asked for cigarettes they were available only if he also made another purchase.

Cairnryan had lost its tranquility and the village soon became a dust basin as heavy lorries churned up roads in their movements to and from the work sites. It became a man's town, a huge labour camp, and could be identified with the kind of activity that surrounded the building of the Forth Bridge.

Various projects were worked on simultaneously but in the beginning there were no stationary boilers to attend. Consequently I was given other work to do, and I found myself chittering at the end of a pneumatic drill preparing ground for a pile construction yard. This was in an area at the northern extremity of the scheme and known as Old House Point. It was remote from the mainstream of the work and our small group laboured contentedly seeing nothing but the occasional vehicle on the road high above the Loch and possibly the passage of the 'Paddy Boat'.

The Deep Water Wharf at Cairn Point was the central piece and the main scene of activity. Two wharfs were to be built here and screw piles were the means of support. These piles were made up of nine feet long cylinders with a diameter of about three feet. The ends of each section had inverted flanges with holes to house one and a quarter inch diameter turned bolts that secured them to each other.

The screw that went into the bed of the loch was not unlike a ship's propellor in appearance with a more pointed centre piece at the bottom. The design of the screw casting at the top was cylindrical and matched the sections that were to be added to it.

Before the screw went into position it was mated with sufficient cylinders to keep the pile above water. A huge floating derrick was then used to place the pile in position. Once in position the same crane hoisted an electric capstan and this was attached by bolts to the upper cylinder on the pile. Screwing operations then commenced and, depending on the strata under the water, progress was fast or otherwise. As the pile sank lower seeking a firm base further sections were added and securing these sections was a hazardous business.

The cylinder sections were picked up by a crane either from the shore or, as the job progressed, from a barge. The rigger then positioned himself on the top of the cylinder section and held on to the crane lifting tackle which was the conventional hook with a piece of wire rope attached. This rope had looped ends which were placed round two bolts slotted into opposing holes on the inverted flanges. When taut the weight of the suspended load forced the bolts at an angle against their temporary housing and held them firm. The cylinder with the rigger atop was then swung high through the air and into position on the screw pile.

Once in position the rigger was then lowered, along with a bag of nuts and bolts and a spanner, into the interior of the pile. The inside flanges were quite narrow and these were used as footrests by the rigger who braced his legs and hips against the inside walls of the cylinder leaving his hands free to work. A man outside directed the crane and hand guided the cylinder section into position. As this manoeuvre was going on the rigger was ready to drop holding bolts into position and when these were in the remaining bolts were placed in the circle of holes and secured with nuts.

This was very dangerous work and although one's body was tight against the inner walls of the cylinder, a wrong move meant a watery grave and no escape, because a fall would be into the water-blocked bowels of the screw. The most frightening time was when the Paddy Boat came close inshore and the pile under construction was hit by the swell. On these occasions the rigger would stop work and brace himself against the inner wall of the swaying pile and pray the thing would hold. This high risk earned only a soldier's pay with possibly a few shillings extra for a trade category.

The screw piles were positioned five abreast and each row was equable and equidistant, 16 feet centres laterally and 20 feet centres longitudinally. Once settled in position the hollow interior of each pile was filled to a depth of four feet six inches with concrete, making a very solid support for the top decking forming the wharf surface.

Work went on day and night in all kinds of weather and the only concession I remember getting was a tot of rum after a very cold night shift. We had a monotonous diet of bread, pilchards and slab cake washed down with plenty of tea brewed on the work site. Loch Ryan must have the biggest stock of fish in Scotland, if we include the hundreds of tins of pilchards deposited there in disgust during the war. The slab cakes, of course, will now be covered in barnacles and will look like the rocks that they were.

Near Old House Point we constructed a jetty, using the more familiar wooden piles. These were hammered into the bed of the loch with a steam hammer suspended from a mobile crane. A huge vertical boiler was installed to provide the steam and I was given the job of stoking the boiler.

I was, in fact, doing the job I had been trained to do.

At the start of the work the steam had but a short distance to travel from the boiler, through lagged piping, to the hammer and we were getting about 30 taps from every head of steam. I would bring the boiler to full pressure, then open the steam valve and the hammering would commence. The sound rebounded from the high embankment carrying the A77 road and echoed across Loch Ryan.

Progress was rapid to start with but as the jetty extended out into the loch the steam delivery pipe had to be lengthened. Consequently the steam hammer had no sooner started when it ran out of steam and spluttered to a stop, so much of the high pressure had condensed in the long pipe. This problem was overcome by putting the boiler on rollers and moving it as the job progressed. The jetty was intended for the transport of beams and slabs to the wharf but weather conditions were unsuitable for regular loading and material eventually went by rail.

On the opposite side of Cairn Point in the direction of Stranraer, wooden piles were used to construct a Lighterage Wharf and these too were hammered home with a steam hammer. Between the Lighterage Wharf and the South Deep Water Wharf at Cairn Point sheet piling was used to shore up land mass and here again a steam hammer was in operation. Once the sheet piles were in position the stretch of water in the vicinity of the two wharfs became a deep anchorage for ocean going ships.

Pre-cast concrete decking was made on site and this job required the skill of steel benders, who shaped the steel frames that gave the decking its strength. These long frames were put together in a yard set aside for the purpose, and a great deal of the work was done in the summer of 1941. In the bright sunshine the steel benders worked stripped to the waist, and although they were Royal Engineers many of them still showed an allegiance to their former regiments, so that we had the unusual sight of craftsmen wearing Glengarrys and Balmorals and possibly a Tank Corps black beret or guardsman's cap. Like people so often do they spoke about the good old days and the camaraderie of their previous Army life and no doubt if they are around today they will feel nostalgic thinking of Cairnryan.

The 931 Port Construction and Repair Company soon developed an identity of its own with Major Earp in the lead and Captain Meirs as his second in command. The Major came from a civil engineering background and his skills were well suited to the work in hand. He could also take on the role of a soldier if need be and it was as a soldier he addressed himself to port construction work.

Captain Meirs dealt mostly with administration and acted very strangely at times. He was keen on discipline and set the pace by example, so much so, that he gave himself seven days CB when he was late on parade one morning. Not only did he confine himself to barracks he also had the Orderly Sergeant drilling him for half an hour each evening, and with a pack on his back, too!

A large Nissen hut served as a Company Office and a similar construction was used as a cookhouse and messroom. Senior NCO's had their own little street of huts near the Company Office and Officers' Mess. The WO1s and 2s were really 'Wimpey's Foremen' in military dress, they knew plenty about piles but little about files, the kind formed on a parade ground.

Arthur Crossman was a corporal in charge of the Orderly Room and although he was a Geordie he had close affiliations with Edinburgh where his wife belonged. He was a very confident person and very outspoken and eventually attained officer rank and served in India. My first proper meeting with him was when he called me into the office and told me he had thrown in the bucket a charge sheet with my name on it.

During one of my leaves from Cairnryan I went to Leeds where I had arranged to meet Dorothy at the station there. I had already bought a suit of blues as a change from drab khaki and wanting to impress my girlfriend I wore these for the occasion. There I was standing at Leeds station and looking very smart when two military policemen approached. I was reprimanded on the spot for wearing dress uniform and they told me, 'The old man here doesn't like it.' This was a reference to whoever was in charge of the military in the Leeds district. An MP took my particulars and I was told to get back into battledress quick.

All this was soon forgotten when Dorothy came on the scene and after a few days together I returned to Cairnryan. It was then Corporal Crossman summoned me to the office and told me about the charge that had come from Leeds—the one he put in the bucket. So, after one year in the Army I had been charged and punished for not doing somebody else's work and charged and not punished for looking too smart!

In December 1941 I went on leave to Edinburgh and was married to Dorothy on Boxing Day. My mates in Hut 29 sent us a telegram of good wishes with a PS for me reading, 'Dinna forget to come back.' I did not forget to go back but I was miserable without my new bride. So, it was arranged that Dorothy would come to Cairnryan and I found accommodation with Mrs. Aitken.

We paid a fair rent for our lodgings but the old postmistress had Dorothy and other guests doing the housework. There were advantages because my wife had access to the wash boiler and other essentials. Still, although near my camp it was not an ideal situation and we looked for a place in Stranraer. For a whole day we trudged the streets searching for a room and by early evening we were beginning to despair when suddenly a black cat jumped from a wall onto my shoulder. Significantly it was my 22nd birthday, May 15th. Sure enough, the next place we tried accepted us and we had a good meal for starters. I applied for, and was granted, a sleeping out pass and from then on we made the best of our few months together c/o 7 Royal Avenue, Stranraer.

Transport to and from work was no problem, there being umpteen Army vehicles passing between Stranraer and Cairnryan. It was rather like being back in civvy street, the only difference being I was always in uniform of some kind. At work it was fatigue dress with the usual army boots, or sometimes rubber boots. We wore a leather jacket to keep out the cold and a cap comforter on the head. Off duty, I was in battledress with the usual heavy boots but in a place like Stranraer there was little need to dress up and evenings by the fire was relaxation enough.

Having my wife beside me relieved me of the temptation to abscond which I did one weekend when Dorothy was in Edinburgh. After tea on a Friday I started out on the road home—hitch-hiking. The first lift I got was in a police car going to Girvan. I sat in the back and to make conversation the police officer sitting beside his driving colleague light-heartedly said, 'I hope you have a pass.' I had nothing but the desire to get home as quickly as possible and I was hoping to catch the last bus or train out of Glasgow.

Lifts came in stages from Girvan to Ayr, from Ayr to Kilmarnock and so into Glasgow, but too late for public transport to Edinburgh. I saw a tramcar heading for Airdrie and jumped aboard. When the conductress came for my fare I spoke to her about the possibility of a lift from Airdrie to Edinburgh. She put me off at a particular spot where there was a chance of newspaper delivery vans passing on their way to the Capital. It was near midnight and the first car to come along was heading for Motherwell, the driver said he would drop me at a junction on the A8 road, the main artery between Glasgow and Edinburgh.

There were traffic lights at this junction and I have found out since that the place was Newhouse. In those days the lights were merely little crosses on a dark background and all around was open country and dense blackout. While waiting for a lift I amused myself by jumping on the rubber strips in the road which had the effect of changing the lights. Then I heard the heavy beat of a diesel motor, but how was the driver going to see me in the pitch darkness—his headlights were also mere crosses. The only way was to light a match and hold it to my face, and this I did.

The lorry that stopped was marked Young's of Leith, and after making my destination known the driver invited me to 'jump in'. 'My,' he said, 'am I glad to see you, I like a bit of company.' He was not half as glad as I was to see him. He dropped me at the end of my street at two o'clock on Saturday morning and Dorothy was more than a little surprised when I told her to 'move over'.

I returned to Cairnryan on Sunday by train via Carlisle and Dumfries avoiding military police at the larger stations, and quietly took up where I had left off, never having been missed from the labour gangs on Loch Ryan.

As the construction work gained momentum more men were drafted to the area and a large camp was established at Drummockloch and another one at Leffnoll, both these places being between Cairnryan and Stranraer and adjacent to Loch Ryan. Stranraer itself had a large Forces settlement and on the west shore of Loch Ryan, in the Kirkcolm area, there was a big RAF base. This was practically opposite Cairn Point and equidistant from Stranraer which was the only town in the area. Consequently hundreds of men looking for entertainment used to converge on Stranraer every Saturday and the place just could not cope. We eventually organised transport and travelled to Girvan or Ayr where there was more room.

Construction of an access railway to No. 2 Military Port began almost simultaneously with that of the port. On the LMS main line one mile east of Stranraer Harbour Junction a siding was installed on the north side of the line. A ground frame was controlled by section tablet. The first occupant was a train of five dormitory coaches and one canteen coach, with steam heating supplied by ex-Highland Railway 4-4-0 Loch Moy. LMS No. 14382, minus internal machinery.

The single siding soon expanded into a large yard of ten parallel roads. On October 11th 1942 the ground frame was replaced by a signalbox named Cairnryan Junction. This was a block post with key token instruments but with no crossing loop on the main line. From the west end of this yard an 'engine escape road' descended at a grade of one in 40 to link up with the head shunt of Stranraer Harbour Junction.

From these exchange sidings the Cairnryan Military Railway was operated by military personnel using engines either owned by or on loan to the War Department. Cairnryan Junction controlled the east end of the yard, the west end being controlled by Aird Block Post, a small erection operating three fixed signals. Here the CMR became single line, curving sharply round to the north and descending steeply for some 1200 yards, half of which was at a gradient of one in 50.

Girder bridges spanned two roads, one leading to Aird Farm, the other being Stranraer's London Road. Just over a mile from Cairnryan Junction was a blockpost at Construction Junction, with fixed signals and a branch trailing in from the west side. At easier grades the line continued its descent to the shore of Loch Ryan, with four level crossings, the fourth being over the A77 road and being protected by pole barriers.

At Invermessan, three miles from the junction, there was a branch to a shipyard, but this was not a blockpost. For the remainder of its course the railway followed the coast, in places on reclaimed ground.

Four miles from the junction the promontory called Leffnoll Point gives a considerable margin to seaward and here was formed the main marshalling yard, with accommodation for 2000 wagons. In this yard trains were broken up into short sections for wharf working. Ground level signalboxes were provided at Leffnoll South and Leffnoll North, with extensive signalling. Leffnoll was also the main locomotive depot.

From Leffnoll South the line became double track. At five and a quarter miles was a smaller yard called School Sidings, again with South and North boxes and signalling. Another half mile brought the railway to a very big layout at Cairn Point, with a fan of sidings serving the berths of the North and South Deep Water Wharfs. Double line ended at Deep Water Quay Block Post at the south end of the sidings. The CMR continued a further mile to its termination on the jetty at Pile Construction Yard. Here were sidings and a small engine shed. Block working ceased beyond Deep Water Quay.

With so many potential customers in the area it was inevitable that the railway should be used for passenger trains. On April 24th, 1942, there arrived a set of close coupled, six wheel non corridor LMS coaches, built at Wolverton in 1911. A timetable was introduced and this provided for a train to Stranraer at 1315 and 1715 on a Saturday and 1851 on other days except Sunday. 'Rubble Bank' at Cairn Point was one terminus and 'Transit' north of the bridge over London Road was the station for Stranraer. In between there were stops at Leffnoll North and Invermessan. The return times from 'Transit' were 2136 and 2306 on a Saturday and 2249 other nights. First and third class accommodation was provided; return fare, third class, from Rubble Bank to Transit was twopence! (As its name implies, Transit was the site of a big transit camp.) Traffic soon outgrew the original coaching stock. On June 21st, 1944, the 2300 from Transit was noted as composed of five bogie coaches of LYR origin, plus three of the Wolverton six wheelers.

In June 1942 King George VI and Queen Elizabeth paid a short visit to Northern Ireland, embarking at Cairnryan's new port. A Royal Train of two vehicles was provided for the journey over the CMR, ex-Caledonian Railway officers' saloon (LMS No. 5018) and a resplendent first class coach. Stranraer shed supplied a 4-4-0, class '2P' No. 600, Driver William Dunlop and Fireman Robert Collins, and on the forenoon of June 24th their Majesties were conveyed to the Lighterage Wharf there to embark on the cruiser HMS *Phoebe*.

War or no war this was a Royal occasion and an honour for the Royal Engineers, and we washed that wharf thoroughly using hoses and hard brushes, and laid out the red carpet.

The Royal Party returned on June 26th and as HMS *Phoebe* sailed up Loch Ryan there was an escort of fighter planes and the ship's company were lined up at attention with cold evening breezes rustling their collars and bell bottoms and chilling their bones. After the King and Queen had disembarked they joined the Royal Train being then hauled by '2P' No. 614, Driver George Harvey of Stranraer. Class 'J69', WD No. 81, ex-LNER No. 7197, preceded the Royal Train in each direction. A temporary stage was erected at Cairnryan Junction for the transfer to the main line Royal Train.

With the departure of the VIP's the men on HMS *Phoebe* were given shore leave until midnight. All at once there seemed to be an invasion of white capped sailors as they rushed up the wharf looking for some entertainment and warmth. We had to tell them there was absolutely nothing of that sort in Cairnryan and the nearest town was six miles away where the pubs closed at 2130. They looked at us in disbelief and when the facts had finally penetrated there were murmurs of derision directed at Scotland with more than a few swear words thrown in. It was a disconsolate crowd that went back aboard the *Phoebe* that night.

Port construction on the scale that was taking place at Cairnryan called for the use of divers for inspection work, and volunteers were invited to apply. James McKechnie, ex-Greenock shipyard worker (carpenter) was a close friend of mine and he lost no time in applying for the job. He was accepted and eventually went to the Royal Navy Diving School at Chatham with some others. On his return he was a qualified diver and gave all his time to what work there was and caring for his diving suit. I learned so much from him I felt I could do the job myself. But going down in the murky waters of Loch Ryan was very different from merely thinking about it.

There was inspection work to be done at the South Deep Water Wharf one day and the diver in his heavy suit was down below, with air bubbles marking his positon. Men of the Pioneer Corps were on the pump which had two handles and was operated like a mangle. Everything seemed to be going well until the German Luftwaffe paid us a rare visit and we were literally attacked 'out of the blue'. Leading the stampede for cover were the two men from the Pioneer Corps and the deserted pump handles could be seen swinging idly. The officer in charge at once realised the serious situation the diver was in and began screaming in rage at the two deserters. He was going to have them shot for running away in face of the enemy. Humbly, and obviously afraid, the men returned to their post and started the pump going again.

Meanwhile the diver was aware of an interruption to his air supply and began to regulate the valve on his helmet. Just then the life supporting air was restored and to a wider valve opening than was desirable. The result was the diver's suit filled with air and became too buoyant for the heavy lead boots to hold down. The diver turned turtle and rushed to the surface feet first striking the bottom of a moored barge. We fished him out quickly and removed his helmet and he just sat there gasping and too dazed to wonder what had happened.

On a construction job like that at Cairnryan accidents seem inevitable and there were many involving equipment and/or personnel. Most were of a minor nature and were caused through inexperience or mismanagement of tools. Crane work was a common source of trouble and if the load was not properly secured it would fall to the ground, or into the water, and bystanders had to be careful not to get in the way. The 'banksman' who attached the load was responsible for ensuring the lifting tackle was properly secured but it was the craneman who dealt with the actual lift and he had to be careful and keep within the crane's lifting limits. He also had to watch the angle of the jib and guard against being pulled over by the load. In between times he had to stoke the boiler fire and keep up the steam pressure.

Benny Blackman was our best crane driver and had experience of the job before joining the Army. He kept everybody right and never made a wrong move. But, Benny could not always be there, and an Army trained crane driver would take over the job on occasions. To the layman the mobile steam crane seemed rather complex and the various levers confusing but to the experienced crane driver the manipulation of the controls became automatic actions.

The relief driver was little more than a layman and every move he made called for deep concentration and deliberate actuation of the levers. He had lifted a nine foot section of screw pile from a stack on the jetty and this was intended to be lowered into a barge. For what seemed an eternity the load hovered over the side of the quay as the crane driver fumbled with the controls, then his right foot inadvertently slipped off the foot brake and the heavy cylinder plummetted to the floor of the barge and nearly to the bed of Loch Ryan, rapidly uncoiling the wire rope lifting tackle from its drum on the crane. Luckily the banksman waiting in the roomy barge to unhook the load moved quickly and suffered only slight shock.

The frustrated crane driver was sacked on the spot and relegated to less responsible work, although I do not think demotion bothered him greatly; Jimmy Bain was the happy-go-lucky type and treated the whole thing lightly. The incident, however, roused my poetic tendencies and youthful exuberance and I wrote the following on one of the cylinder sections stacked on the quay.

38

Here lies the body of Jimmy Bain
Who tried to work a mobile crane
He wanted to drive like Benny Blackham
But the guvner got wise and had to sack 'im.

This brought smiles to many faces, including that of the officer who sacked poor Jimmy.

There was sadness, too, at Cairnryan and we all felt a sense of grief when a mobile crane went into the drink taking the driver to his death. His mistake had been allowing the jib to over-reach with the result that the suspended load pulled the crane over the edge of the quay.

The men who operated the tugs and barges at Cairnryan came from the Thames area in family units, many of them related to each other. They seemed immune to Army discipline but as lightermen they knew their job thoroughly. These were the men who positioned the barges and moved the floating derricks to new positions. Their Cockney humour was infectious and their team spirit left nothing to be desired. Left alone to do the job they knew best they were happy to get on with it, but when our OC took it into his head that we were going soft and ordered us to climb over the hills above our camp (cooks included—no exceptions) it was then the Cockneys said some rude things about Scotland.

The first vessel to make use of Cairnryan as a port was the *Revelly*, which brought a cargo of timber from Canada. This was discharged in the stream and rafted ashore. On May 7th, 1943 the Candian-built *Fort McLaughlin*, of 7129 tons gross, berthed at Cairnryan and loaded a full cargo of military equipment, sailing on May 15th. In the months which followed, 25 ships of somewhat similar tonnage were loaded and dispatched. A list, admittedly incomplete, shows 18 ships arriving from New York and discharging their entire cargoes at Cairnryan. Numerous coasting vessels visited the port and each morning a full cargo of milk arrived from Larne. The milk train, sometimes as many as 25 vans, was worked to Cairnryan Junction by WD engines, and thence to Glasgow by LMSR. The empties were returned in the evening. But I never saw the cargo ships and the milk trains, the 931 Port Construction and Repair Company was given its marching orders in July 1942 when I had been nearly two years in the Army.

In all great engineering projects, just as in life itself, problems are a continual challenge. So it was that in September 1942 the sappers at Cairnryan had to deal with a quite unexpected difficulty.

While pile driving was going on at the South Deep Wharf work was held up because of an obstruction which divers identified as the hull of a sunken vessel. Fate could surely not have chosen a more opportune time for the recovery of a ship's cargo which was lost nearly 60 years before, when the vessel went to the bottom of Loch Ryan.

It was on the morning of Monday, February 19th, 1883 that the three masted barque *Falcon* with 500 tons of coal aboard for South America went on fire. Everything possible was done to extinguish the flames but the vessel continued to burn until the evening, when she sank.

Years passed and in time the loss of the ship was forgotten; then came the Royal Engineers prodding at the grave of the *Falcon*, which for 59 years had been gradually sinking into the sand and silt. Operations were begun to remove the coal, and soon the whole cargo was retrieved in good condition, much to the delight of the Minister of Fuel.

What remained of the vessel was blown up, thus allowing construction work to proceed.

In later years the harbour was used extensively by the United States Forces for bringing in weapons and material from America. These were transported by road and rail to England in preparation for the invasion of Europe and, for a long time, the quiet roadways of Galloway echoed to the sound of strange tongues and strange noises as the convoys forged their way southwards.

Then came the end of the war. The dread emergency of a major port being put completely out of action had not taken place. Cairnryan had doubtless taken some of the weight, but it had never been worked to capacity. Now it was left—this fine port with its elaborate equipment, far distant from bombing activity in wartime, but equally distant from industrial activity in peace. There were, of course, bright ideas for its future use. A most obvious idea was to switch the terminal of the cross-channel service from Stranraer to Cairnryan. There was instant protest from the town of Stranraer, and the project was dropped. In August 1945 came the first train of gas shells, which were loaded onto large cargo vessels, these being taken out to the Atlantic and scuttled, a destroyer taking off the crew after the sea cocks had been opened. Four such ships were dispatched in 1945, one in 1946, one in 1947 and one in 1955.

In the course of time the supply of old ships gave out and the useless ammunition was taken out to sea on landing craft and dumped overboard. For a time the harbour installations were used by the Ministry of Supply as a centre for ship-breaking. A firm from Clydeside carried out the work and among the battleships that were reduced to scrap were the *Ramillies* and the *Valiant*.

The depot ship *Sandhurst* lay at the harbour during the early post-war period, when a fleet of U-boats which had been surrendered by the

The former LMS college, Derby, where sappers were trained to operate military railways. Here it was I found myself designated 'Stationary Engine Attendant', not quite what I had expected.

Siddals Road Barracks, Derby, 8.9.40. Sergeant Major Brown poses with a new batch of recruits including three from Edinburgh. Author third from left, back row. Tom Campbell fifth from left, back row. Bob Henderson looking over SMs right shoulder. Fothergill is third from right, back row. Bill Shorocks fourth from left, front row. Some of these sappers are still carrying civilian gas masks.

Merryweather Pump, otherwise known as 'Valiant' because of its introduction by the captain of that ship in 1880. These pumps were widely used by the sappers in the South African war and the two world wars. They were also used by bomb disposal sappers to supply steam for trepanning machine and for boiling out explosive from UXB. This was the contraption that brought about my first charge in the Army—at Weston Quarry in 1940.

Cairnryan, the peaceful village on the east shore of Lock Ryan before an army of sappers arrived to build No. 2 Military Port.

Loch Ryan, Stranraer, and the Cairnryan Military Railway connecting with the LMSR.

Port construction work at Cairnryan—sappers marching on to the job. Large marshalling yard right looking north towards Girvan.

Screw piles as used at Cairnryan.

A 'Screwrite' cylinder base ready for screwing into the bed of Loch Ryan.

Cairnryan, South Deep Water Wharf looking towards Stranraer. Though never used for the purpose intended this centre piece of No. 2 Military Port came to be the last resting place of some famous warships; Ramilies, Valiant, Hermes, Eagle *and* Ark Royal, *to name but a few.*

Ark Royal *at Cairnryan ready for the hammer.*

Cairnryan: HMS Eagle *runs aground while being manoeuvred to her berth at the South Deep Water Wharf prior to scrapping.*

Cairnryan: the view from the Stranraer/Larne ferry showing F125 waiting to be broken up. On the South Deep Water Wharf can be seen scrap from Ark Royal and out of sight is HMS Blake, silently awaiting her end. Above the village at centre of picture are the Nissen huts of the camp used by the 931 Port Construction and Repair Company RE during WW2.

Cairnryan: Lighterage Wharf, now used by car ferries serving Northern Ireland. King George VI and Queen Elizabeth, after a visit to Ulster, disembarked here on June 26th, 1942 from HMS Phoebe.

Eastbourne, Green Street. Police, firemen and the army attend the aftermath of the German 'hit and run' tactics. The air raid warden on the left of the picture is William Tyhurst, our landlord during my sojourn at Eastbourne.

Eastbourne, Beach Road. Devastation after a visit from the Luftwaffe. This was close to where I comforted Mrs. Tyhurst under the staircase at 'No. Sixty'. There was something eerie about these ravaged buildings during my lonely vigil on fire picket at night.

Germans were anchored in the loch. Ammuniton dumping went on intermittently for years after the war, with the Navy, Army and RAF all sharing in the activities. By the spring of 1959 the work of the Services came to an end and about 300 civilians who had been employed at the port were gradually dismissed. The closing of the war-time harbour raised the number of workless to a high figure and Stranraer was classed as a development area. Efforts were made in many directions and by many people to have the harbour taken over by a private firm and this was eventually done. In the early part of 1960 a start was made with the changeover, but little had been achieved by the end of 1962 and disappointment was being felt at the long delay.

So far as the CMR was concerned, the signalling equipment was dismantled in 1956. The War Department left Cairnryan in April 1959, and the last of the WD rolling stock was taken away. No fewer than 32 engines are known to have worked on the CMR. Most numerous were the LNER 0-6-0 tanks, with 'J50' Nos. 1058, 3157, 3160 and 3219, 'J67' No. 7169 and 'J69' Nos. 7058, 7081, 7088, 7168, 7197, 7344 and 7362. There were seven GWR 'Dean Goods', Nos. 2399, 2430, 2433, 2470, 2517, 2536 and 2545. A brief visit was paid by SR 0-8-0 tank No. 951. 'Austerity' classes were represented by 2-8-0s 7223 and 7241, 2-10-0s by 3798-9, and 0-6-0 tanks by 71531, 75018, 75048 and 75049. There were two USA types, 2-8-0 No. 2640 and 0-6-0 tank No. 1943. An 0-6-0 tank, Walter Scott, (Maning Wardle 1237/1892) and a diesel 0-4-0 (Barclay 356/1941) complete the catalogue.

The demolishing of the railway was completed and on December 30th, 1962 Cairnryan Junction box was closed, though a connection to the CMR remained some years thereafter. The ruins of railway and port became a sad sight. At the end of 1969 four cranes, probably rusted and useless, were left, and four lonely men kept watch over the silent wharves and grass-grown tracks of an enterprise of war for which a time of peace had no use.

The dead backwater seemed ideally suited for a graveyard and in recent years a shipbreaking firm has made it just that. Here it was in the early seventies that the aircraft carrier HMS *Hermes* was reduced to scrap and in 1979 HMS *Eagle* awaited the same fate at Cairnryan. This aircraft carrier was reluctant to be tied up at Cairn Point Deep Water Wharf and defiantly ran aground. When the massive hulk eventually settled into its last resting place it disrupted television viewing in the village every time it rose with the tide. HMS *Ark Royal* also died at Cairnryan in 1981/82.

Chapter Four

Our destination was Eastbourne and an advance party had already gone there to organise accommodation, etc. Army trucks took the main body of men to Stranraer Town Station where we boarded a special train for the 'Suntrap of the South', as the Sussex coastal town is now called. As Cairnryan receded in the distance I had mixed feelings about the place. I had been in on the start of a great undertaking and I was somewhat disappointed that I was not going to be there to see the great port fully operational. Somehow the hard work and the misery of the place never came to mind and I could only think of the happier times we had shared. 'No. 2 Military Port' was a complex and elaborate composition, an unfinished symphony, but I had no doubt that the labour legions left behind would finish the job we had begun.

Dorothy was at the station to see me off, another parting in our short married life, and for how long? Who could tell? We had known but a few months of blessed happiness and the years have not dimmed the joys we eagerly grasped. We lived for each day knowing that the morrow might well be the start of a long separation. Our memories are made of simple things like the slab cakes and tins of pilchards I used to smuggle home hidden in the spaciousness of my battledress. These food items may have been a monotonous diet to the port builders, but to the hard pressed civilians they were a treat. It was in that room at Stranraer I first knew the fireside comfort of the married state, although the home was not ours to call our own and security just did not exist. It was in that room our first child was conceived, so, Stranraer with all its failings, will always have a place in our hearts.

As the long train snakishly struggled over the tortuous terrain to Dumfries and the south I tried to console myself by anticipating a new life style in Eastbourne. My mates, too, were a happy crowd and soon stopped me from wearying. At Carlisle my compartment stopped directly opposite the cab of a great Pacific locomotive and looking down at me was Dave Stewart, an old colleague from St. Margaret's. We exchanged pleasantries and jokingly talked about changing jobs. I do not know what Dave's reaction would have been had it been possible but I was all for it. I would have loved to have gone back to civvy street that day and been re-united with my wife.

Although we did not have to change trains it was a long slow journey to Eastbourne where we arrived early next day. We marched in brilliant sunshine from the station to Royal Parade, our new address. I had never before been as far south but I knew the place had changed for the worse since the carefree pre-war days. The sound of our marching feet echoed through the emptiness of the fine hotels facing the sea and window shutters banged ominously reminiscent of a prelude to some Karloff horror scene.

Barbed wire entanglements were a menacing division between promenade and beach and the pleasure pier was deserted and terribly neglected. We had arrived at the height of the holiday season, but now the once happy crowds were only an apparition, Eastbourne was a ghost town.

A house in Royal Parade became our Company Office and farther along to the east other empty buildings were used for billets. The fish market opposite was transformed into a cookhouse and messroom and the Heatherleigh Hotel on the Marine Parade was also taken over as billets. Some hotels on Grand Parade were occupied by Army and RAF and the Grand Hotel, famous for its pre-war Palm Court Orchestra, was occupied by WAAFS. This hotel received a direct hit during an air raid and there were many casualties.

Any ideas we had about lazing on the beach and bathing in the Channel were cancelled out by the fact that the sands were infested with death dealing anti-personnel mines. As if to emphasise the danger lurking on our doorsteps a dog that strayed onto the beach was blown to smithereens not far from the Beach Hotel and this was the fate of many dogs that had been abandoned by their evacuated owners. Eastbourne was a restricted area for obvious reasons; the '931' was now in the front line!

We were not at that time aware of our new mission in life but we set out to explore the sparsely populated town and soon found the Winter Gardens with Gordon Rider and his band still holding out. The Anniversary Waltz was in the Top Ten at that time and, with sentiment, I recalled the day in Stranraer when Dorothy and I were looking for lodgings and found a warm togetherness as we stood on a show ground listening to the strains of that emotional tune. When Gordon Rider announced the next dance as a waltz, followed by those familiar opening bars, I longed to take the floor with my wife. Such pleasure was denied me but I could give vent to my feelings by singing and I went across to Gordon Rider whose brushes were caressing his drums with feather light touches.

I asked him in a whisper if I could sing and he beamed and eagerly

43

beckoned me onto the stage. My cue was only seconds away but as I stood facing the microphone and gazed down on the swaying couples in that darkened ballroom I knew deep down this was my song, this was my night. The sentimental words matched the mood of the moment and I think the dancers guessed the song had real meaning for me. Gordon Rider certainly guessed it because he signalled for two violinists to take up position at my side and by the time I repeated the refrain I knew I had never sung so well before and I would never quite match the performance again. From then on, whenever that song was played at the Winter Gardens, Gordon Rider always looked for my approach to the stage.

My philosophy in life has always been, 'when in doubt—brew up', but whenever the Chief Royal Engineer was in doubt as to how to keep men gainfully employed he, in his wisdom, opted for military training. This was our fate at Eastbourne and we were introduced to the kind of stuff Commandos thrive on. There was physical training for half an hour before breakfast. An assault course was rigged up to test our endurance. There was square bashing, rifle drill, bayonet fighting, Bren gun and anti tank gun training, field works, demolition work, mine disposal, route marches—the lot. Oh yes, and when we had time we were given lectures on a variety of subjects.

Bob French, an ex-regular in the Cameronians, was one of our instructors whose speciality was drill and bayonet fighting. The fact that he was an Edinburgh man found no favours as far as I was concerned. He was mean and ugly and his approach to militarism was that of a fanatic. If he was lacking in trade qualifications he more than earned his three stripes by his dedication to the Army; he was a good soldier.

On bayonet fighting his ugly, wart covered face would be screwed up in the most grotesque form as he demonstrated how to effectively pierce the dummy. 'You're going to kill the Germans,' he would yell, 'not kiss them!' and, with that, he would throw the rifle and bayonet back to the man he had borrowed it from. Then he would rant on with, 'Now, get lined up there again and do it the way I showed you. If you lot ever have to face the enemy, heaven help you—and us.' And so he would go on and on and on. Eventually, a window would open in the barrack room he had for a brain and his military indoctrinated mind would yield to humanity and his despaired pupils. 'Awe right,' he would growl, 'have a smoke.'

Sitting on the grass with a captive audience of mostly conscripted men, Bob would talk of his experiences with the Army in India and warm to the subject as he related the events which led to the scuttling of thousands of rifles in the Bay of Bengal, when Britain disarmed between the wars. He was incensed at our unpreparedness for Hitler's war and the fact that we at Eastbourne were scraping the barrel for weapons to train with. But, his reminiscences were abruptly halted when he realised half his audience

44

was asleep and the other half was nodding and he would shout, 'Right lads, back to the battlefield, and for goodness sake try a bit harder this time.'

Very often the whole company was out drilling in Royal Parade, which was aptly named for the purpose. Under the watchful eye of CSM Charlie Martin, we would 'right wheel' and 'left wheel', 'about turn', and 'open order, march'. Charlie was a big man and in contrast to the sergeant major image, his orders came from his larynx and not from his belly. His six feet five inches frame was always erect, but on parade he could stretch this a few more inches. Not only was his body stretched to the limit, his fingers, too, reacted to his every command and would extend downwards and recoil like a yo-yo.

Major Earp sometimes looked in on our performance and would stand to attention on the pavement, gripping tightly the officer's stick under his right oxter. But one day he decided to lend a hand in the performance and marched by our side egging us on. 'Keep in line! Swing those arms! Left, right, left, right, left,' he yelled and to demonstrate what was expected of us he walked sideways by my right flank, grasping my arm with both of his hands and pushing it to the high horizontal position, front and back. 'C'mon, Meacher,' he said, 'swing them!' And all the while the stick was still under his oxter.

At that time the German hit and run raiders struck at Eastbourne continuously. Fighter planes would cross the Channel at near zero altitude, just clear of the water, so as to avoid the Radar defences. They circled the town, dropping bombs and machine gunning and were back in France before the dust settled.

At other places there was a period of time between the siren wailing and the actual air raid and people had a chance to take shelter. In Eastbourne there was a 'cuckoo' warning which, as the name implies, sounded like that migratory bird. When this sound was heard people knew the enemy was on the doorstep. More often than not the attacks on the south coast were surprise raids and our section got the biggest surprise of its life one sunny August day.

We were billeted in the Heatherleigh Hotel about a quarter of a mile from the fish market messroom. At meal times we paraded under any NCO who happened to be there and we marched at ease to the dining hall. We each had two white plates, knife, fork and spoon and we sang and were generally noisy as we went on our way.

It was then the Focke-Wulf 190s arrived, coming in behind the pier and the first thing the German pilots saw was all those white plates glinting in the sun against the contrasting khaki uniforms. Instead of making a wide circle of the town as they usually did they made direct for the 'plate platoon' with machine guns blazing.

We realized the danger just as the roar of the planes came into earshot with their change of direction and the plates went up in the air as we dived into hotel areas for protection. Masonry fell about us as the gun fire sprayed the buildings and we huddled there with the expectancy of doomed men. In a matter of seconds it was all over and we reformed ranks on the promenade, minus a lot of plates but unharmed otherwise. We had to borrow plates from other people until such time as we acquired replacements for the pieces littering the promenade.

There was danger, too, from the sea as great waves delivered flotsam and jetsam onto the beaches, not the usual kind of rubbish from ships and elsewhere, but death dealing sea mines with their dreaded projections. These could bob about on the waves for hours threatening the whole area and people had to be evacuated. If the mine became stranded on the beach the RN disposal people could possibly get rid of this menace. But the Navy men were unable to stop one of these monsters crashing against Eastbourne pier and causing extensive damage and mass evacuation.

Quick firing Bofor guns were in action along the seafront in a feeble attempt to deter the enemy. Our own contribution to the defence of Eastbourne was twin Bren guns on a Motley mounting on the roof of the cookhouse. Farther across town some Canadians had a similar arrangement and were, in fact, successful in bringing down a raider. Local people had a collection for the 'on target' men.

After some intensive tuition from Sergeant French a few of us were considered capable of using a Bren gun. It certainly was not the Sergeant's fault if we were not, he had us dismantling and assembling the gun blindfolded. Then came the day when I climbed to the cookhouse roof and took up my position behind the twin Brens.

The weather was damp and Eastbourne was shrouded in sea-mist; a rubber groundsheet protected the guns. I wore an overcoat and tin hat and sat comfortably in the swivel chair hoping that action would never be imminent, let alone reality. There were binoculars for use in scanning the sky but visibility was minimal and the glasses hung round my neck. Looking over towards Beachy Head I could see the vague outline of a plane moving slowly towards me through the fog. I recalled my lessons in aircraft recognition, but in the classroom the planes were on bright posters and capable of being recognised by their silhouette and full form. All I was seeing coming closer was the mere shadow, or semblance, of an aircraft. As it came near I could see it was practically at roof level then all at once and for fleeting seconds it was directly opposite my gun emplacement and I was staring at a black cross on a big fuselage. The German pilot and tail gunner seemed no farther away than across a table and they were smiling and waving to me. I was swamped by flooding impulses and felt powerless to make a move. It was too late to train the guns on a near sitting target, I should have been lining up the Brens as the plane approached. By the time I had removed the protective cover and swung into action Jerry would possibly have been near Dover. They seemed to be on a reconnaissance visit and had the freedom to reconnoitre, because not one gun opened up.

I consoled myself with the thought that had I fired, the intruder might have retaliated and I learned later many people were like-minded, they had had enough punishment without asking for more. It also occurred to me that I would have had the guns to clean and the quartermaster would have been there counting the empty cartridges before replenishing the 100 round drum magazines. In fact, I would have been somewhat disturbed and my two hour sojourn on the revolving gun seat would have been less pleasant.

We slept on palliasses laid out on the floor in rooms bare of furniture. Heatherleigh was the biggest billet and although the rooms were empty there was a billiard table in the basement and we had the use of this. The owner of the hotel, a woman, visited the place occasionally and she was very friendly and seemed interested in our welfare. Her main interest, however, was in the hotel and its post-war future and she used to hint about the damage done to the floors by our hobnail boots. The sound of our heavy feet echoed through the empty rooms and, seemingly mindful of our health, the lady would suggest we wore plimsolls.

The Officers' Mess was at the western end of Grand Parade, well past the pier and remote from the main activity. I had friends working in the kitchen there and would call in after visiting Jim McKechnie who spent most of his time in a back street garage cleaning and airing his diving suit. On 19th August 1942 I was out on such a jaunt and all that day, from early morning, wave after wave of Allied planes headed out over the Channel towards the French coast and Dieppe. Many of them, less purposeful, limped back to England again.

In the kitchen of the Officers' Mess it was early evening and we could hear the 'thud, thud' of exploding bombs from across the Channel. We were not fully aware of the significance of the event but we knew men were risking their lives and many were dying. The waiters moved quickly to and fro between the kitchen and dining room serving dinner, and at one point while the door was ajar I could hear Major Earp speaking loudly in anger. This was followed by the return to the kitchen of a very subdued waiter carrying a plate and when I asked what all the fuss was about the waiter screwed up his face and said, 'Oh, his soup's cold!' So, while brave Canadians were dying and going into captivity at Dieppe, the OC 931 Port Construction and Repair Company was having tantrums about his cold soup.

I had not been long in Eastbourne when I was planning to get Dorothy beside me. Being a restricted zone it was necessary to obtain permission and a visitor's permit from the appropriate authority. This essential document was applied for and granted, but I still had to get a sleeping out pass. My application for this was rejected but, to his credit, Major Earp called me to his office and explained why. 'Supposing,' he said, 'this company was in real trouble, the enemy had landed and we have our backs to the wall. At a time when the situation is desperate and I need every man available you will, naturally, be running to look after your wife. So, you see, Meacher, I just cannot give you a sleeping out pass—I'm sorry.'

That was it, the short interview was over and I found myself out in the street again. I went straight to a nearby post office and bought a letter card and wrote to Dorothy telling her to come to Eastbourne. I never thought about the consequence, I was in love and love would find a way.

At about that time two Canadian sergeants came to instruct us on anti-personnel mines. On the way to the open air lecture site at the end of Royal Parade these courageous fellows made a gap in the barbed wire entanglements barring access to the beach and dug up a mine from the sand. They then proceeded to dismantle the thing as they described its design and lethal efficiency. After re-assembly the mine was returned to its hole in the beach and covered with sand and gravel.

From here we adjourned to a grassy spot where we sat down for a lecture on the intricacies of the anti-personnel mine. The real business was over and we were talking amongst ourselves when the Company Runner came on the scene. He came direct to me and quietly told me my wife was in a small tearoom in Beach Road near its junction with Royal Parade. I asked the Canadian in charge for permission to leave and this he readily agreed to.

It was great to see Dorothy again and we lost no time in looking for digs. With so many empty places in Eastbourne finding a room was not difficult and life began to be meaningful. As soon as the Orderly Officer and Orderly Sergeant had passed on their rounds each night I passed along the quiet back streets of Eastbourne to our warm nest. Love had found a way!

We were not long bedded down one night when the peace was rudely disturbed and Eastbourne was getting another hammering. These surprise attacks were nerve-shattering and this was Dorothy's first experience of the hellish business. We held each other close and prayed that we would survive and when calm was restored we went outside with others to assess the damage.

It was a warm night and we wore only our sleeping attire. In our peril we felt a close affinity with complete strangers, the like of which we never

48

knew before and have never known since. Drifting white clouds were like stepping stones to a big moon aloft in a star studded sky and we could see volumes of dust settling on streets less fortunate than ours. A few more empty acres had been created, a few more families dissipated.

Soon after this raid Dorothy moved to 60 Beach Road, and the motherly affection of Mrs. Tyhurst, who soon became 'Auntie Ty'. She lived with her husband Will, who was an Air Raid Warden in his spare time. Apart from taking Dorothy in, room was also found for Joyce Crossman and baby daughter, family of Arthur Crossman, who was by this time a sergeant in the Company office. The Tyhursts' only son, Frank, was a Petty Officer on HMS *Indomitable* somewhere at sea. 'Sixty' Beach Road was but a stone's throw from Royal Parade, and Dorothy could stand on the doorstep and watch me going through my paces.

It was an open secret that my wife was in our midst in defiance of Major Earp's ruling. Admittedly, he could not stop us having visitors, but he could stop sleeping out passes, and did so. The OC, however, never caused me any trouble, my few difficulties were created by Sergeant French.

The Company transport vehicles were parked in a yard in the built up area not too far from HQ and eight sentries and an NCO guarded this place at night. I had to take my turn at this duty and lose out on home comforts, but not completely. I would arrange things so that I was last on sentry turn and, since the guard was mounted at 1800 hours, this meant I had until midnight before I was required. But things nearly came unstuck one night.

My friend Bob French was Orderly Sergeant and after he had mounted the guard he went away to attend to other things. I immediately winked to the other lads and made my way through the back streets to Auntie Ty's house. Soon I was sitting in comfort by the fire with my wife and Auntie Ty. I had not been sitting long when a knock came to the front door and when our landlady opened the door I could hear the loud voice of Sergeant French enquiring about Sapper Meacher. I immediately went through the back door and raced back to the guardroom and joined my mates, who were eating fish suppers. My breathing was still rather heavy when Sergeant French rushed in. 'Where have you been?' he demanded of me. I quietly turned and looked up at him, feigning surprise. 'Me?' I said. 'I've been away for fish suppers.'

The sergeant's mouth fell open in surprise and sheer disbelief, but there was no way of finding out where I had been and I knew Mrs. Tyhurst was on my side. Furthermore, somebody had to go for the fish suppers. Bob never bothered me again that night and I quickly resumed my fireside chat with more congenial companions. Also, Tommy

Handley and Itma was on the wireless, not to mention Auntie Ty's excellent supper.

Entrance to Heatherleigh was by way of a short flight of steps which opened out onto a small balcony and the front door. Inside, on the right, there was a fairly large room which I shared with Jim McKechnie and some others. This was my official Army quarter. While room-mates slept on the floor my palliasse had been discarded and replaced by a single bed, a white hospital bed which Mrs. Tyhurst had loaned to me. However, I had no need for a bed in Heatherleigh while Dorothy was at Beach Road, so Jim McKechnie slept in the hospital bed and I lay, fully clothed, under the top blanket of his bed until the roll call was past. Then I would slip out a back window, down a drainpipe and hurry through the back streets to Beach Road and Dorothy.

It was after lights out when the Orderly Sergeant went on his rounds and as usual I lay in McKechnie's bed fully dressed listening to the approaching footsteps. The room door opened and the darkness was pierced with blinding torchlight. The beam of light swung over every bed and came to rest on my face. I moved my head away and mumbled in mock protest and I could see the light searching the area round my bed, then it steadied full on my face.

Through half closed eyes I could see the bizarre face of Sergeant French beyond the light and I got some idea what is in store for a child who is threatened with the 'bogieman'. 'You b----- you!' exclaimed the sergeant. 'I believe you're lying there with your clothes on,' and with that he pulled back the blanket. There I was, fully clothed, battledress, gaiters, ammunition, boots—the lot. Mr. French had obviously been suspicious when no clothes could be seen lying by my bed and his suspicions were confirmed when he pulled back that blanket.

I listened to his heavy feet going through all the rooms upstairs and the noise was amplified by the bareness of the place. Then came the clatter as he came down the stairs and it was only when he had passed through the front door that the noise receded. I lay there for a few minutes giving him time to get well away then I went through the back window and disappeared in the blackout. There was no follow up to this incident and I knew then Bob French's bark was worse than his bite.

Even when the time came for Sergeant French to put me on a charge, I bore him no ill will. From the Army's point of view I had been negligent and it is only now, when looking back over the years, I find the incident amusing.

The weather was quite cold and we wore overcoats as we paraded for guard duty outside Heatherleigh. Lieutenant Robertson (a Geordie) was the Orderly Officer and French the Orderly Sergeant. The ex-Cameronian really came into his own when he was in charge of a quasi-

ceremonial parade. He really barked out the orders, 'Guard—'Shun!'
'Open Order—March!' 'Guard will fix bayonets—guard, Fix!'

The preliminary command 'Guard will fix bayonets' found all of us
drill perfect and we stood with our feet together and rifle, with butt on
the ground, held at the full extent of our left arm, our right hand gripping
the bayonet handle in an upturned scabbard. At the command 'Fix' the
bayonets were withdrawn in unison and slapped smartly onto the end of
the rifle, that is, all except Meacher's. My withdrawal was retarded and
there was an exhibition of tugging rather than fast, smooth extraction.
French was fuming at the idea of his parade being ruined by one man,
his face was white and saliva oozed from his mouth. He was, in fact,
foaming at the mouth.

When I saw my bayonet on the end of the rifle it was red with rust and
I realised it had been replaced in the scabbard in a wet condition after a
bayonet fighting session in the rain.

Then came the command, 'Guard—'Shun!' and the rifles were drawn
smartly into our sides. As I stood to attention waiting to be inspected I
pulled hard on the rifle stock hoping that the rusty bayonet would be
hidden in the shoulder folds of my overcoat. But it was not to be, there
was no hiding place.

Lieutenant Robertson, if he had not already done so, quickly spotted
the sad state of my bayonet but did not make a great fuss about it.
Sergeant French was speechless and we had mounted guard and were
relaxing before he approached me to obtain details for the charge sheet.
I do not think he even spoke the word 'charge', it went without saying
that was the obvious way to deal with the situation. The only way, in fact.

I did not like being in trouble, but now that I was in trouble I accepted
it and I sensed a tone of pity in French's voice as he spoke quietly to me.
It often happens that when it comes to the crunch all the previous threats
pale in significance and are seen for what they are, just a load of wind.
The ultimate had been achieved and I think the 'hard man' French was
more than a wee bit sorry.

My appearance before the OC coincided with my being posted on
detachment to Acrise, near Folkestone. It was all over in a few minutes
and the punishment was 'seven days stoppage of pay'. The truck taking
our party to Acrise waited for me outside the office and we were off as
soon as I climbed aboard. My last sight of Royal Parade included Dorothy
and Sergeant French standing together waving me goodbye.

My new address was Watney House, Acrise Place, near Folkestone, but
we still used the Eastbourne address in our letter headings and for the
receipt of mail. Watney House was a rambling brick mansion stuck miles
from anywhere, the property of the brewing family. At Acrise we came
under the Dover Command and were just about in range of the German

guns which regularly shelled Dover.

Like Heatherleigh, there was no furniture in Watney House and in the basement there were big empty kitchens. However, we were expert at improvising and soon organised a meal service and those with aptitude took on the job of cooking. We slept on the usual palliasses in spacious rooms which were draughty but tolerable.

Our job at Acrise was to cut down brushwood and tie this into bundles using wire, the tool for the job being a billhook. These bundles were transported by road to the railhead where they were transhipped into rail vehicles and forwarded to Newhaven. Here there was another detachment working on new slipways for invasion barges. The brushwood was sunk into the mud and this was covered by ashes and rubble and on top of this went a thick layer of concrete. So, as early as October 1942 work was underway for the Allied invasion of France. The Royal Engineers were living up to their reputation of being 'first in the field and last to leave'.

It was a long walk from Watney House to our place of work and there was no question of marching—all that was behind us at Eastbourne. We just walked casually along a bridle-path through wooded country shrouded in early morning mist. It was hard work, but nobody stood over us and NCOs and sappers shared the effort. We dressed as we had done in Cairnryan and shaving was optional.

Most of our leisure time was spent in Watney House reading, or writing or playing some kind of game. It was late autumn and the evenings were closing in. But we did make an effort to go further afield at weekends and our first outing is readily recalled. There were four of us, including Jim McKechnie.

We crossed some fields in brilliant moonlight and went to a village dance. This was held in a big wooden building, probably the village hall. Catch phrases in those days were just as popular as they are today and our pet saying was, 'Are you the Naafi manager?' Where it originated I do not know and 40 years on it sounds silly, but at the time it caused a laugh and it was good to laugh. Anyway, we had fun dancing and meeting girls again, but other soldiers seemed to object to us enjoying ourselves and as time passed it was obvious they were looking for trouble. Their shoulder insignia was a tree and these trees were all over the place.

At the interval, Jim McKechnie voiced what we were all thinking, that is, there was trouble brewing for the sappers. It was arranged that we all disappeared quietly, one at a time and rendezvous clear of the village and get back to Watney House quick. I watched the others go out while I was dancing and when the music stopped and I walked off the floor I just kept walking through the exit.

On my way down the road I encountered a small circle of people and looking closer I saw it was McKechnie engaged in fisticuffs with one of the 'tree' soldiers. I stopped to look on and was ready to go to my mate's assistance if need be. I had only been standing a minute when the 'tree' soldier turned away from McKechnie and punched me in the face. With that he ran off, with me in hot pursuit, but before I could get my revenge the other sappers were calling for me to join them and get away quick, the 'tree men' were after our blood.

The four of us ran together over the fields until we were sure there was nobody following. When we stopped Jim had a look at my face and in the moonlight he could see my left eye was a mess and I was beginning to feel it too. Back at Watney House we went down to the cookhouse and Jim stood me against a wall and applied a piece of cold meat to the injured eye. At that, I just slid down the wall in a dead faint.

Next day at work my eye looked grim but luckily there was no one but my mates to see it and to them it was a great joke. Later in the week Lieutenant Robertson visited us and he, too, was amused at my misfortune, which I explained to him was the result of my encounter with a tree. I did not elaborate and tell him what kind of tree.

Not long after this incident a few of us were recalled to Eastbourne where Dorothy was still in residence. Our replacements at Acrise included Sergeant French, and it was sad to see this proud soldier reduced to the servility of woodcutting. Our return to HQ was for the purpose of augmenting the labour force at Newhaven and we travelled to and from this Channel port each day. The fact that I had been at Acrise, however, was not forgotten and just before Christmas 1942, on 24th December to be exact, I was given the job of delivering Christmas fare to my friends in the woods. It was not just a case of jumping on a train or bus, my movements in this restricted area had to be authorised and for this reason I was issued with Army Form 01735.

The 'Authority' was OC Unit and under the heading Regimental Route (For use only when billets are not required) the following was printed:

'It is his Majesty's pleasure that you do cause the Troops under your command in so far as authorised by the King's Regulations and Orders for the Army, to proceed from time to time, as occasions shall require, by which routes as you may judge expedient to or from such place or places as shall be necessary in the performance of their duties.

Given at the War Office, this
22nd day of April 1942
By His Majesty's Command
Signed P. J. Grigg'

Then followed, under my number and name, typewritten details of my destination, the reason for my journey, the train and bus service to be used in both directions, dress to be worn and instructions to draw haversack rations from the cookhouse. Oh yes, and I had to report back to the Company Office on my return. On the reverse side of the form there was space for details of warrants issued and charges incurred.

The Christmas fare included cigarettes and chocolate and other delicacies and there was a sum of money from the Unit funds for the purchase of beer. I looked upon the trip as an opportunity for a day out and a nice change and although Dorothy was in an advanced state of pregnancy I took her with me.

We travelled to Folkestone by train and guided by the 'Regimental Route' form, took a bus to the Black Horse Inn where the Acrise Place road joins the A260 leading onto the main Dover to Canterbury Road. On leaving the bus we were, as I well knew we would be, right in the country. It was a long walk to Watney House and farther still to the work site where the men would be at that time of day, 11 o'clock in the morning. Dorothy had to rest with her 'load' more than once but eventually we reached Watney House, which was deserted. I took the opportunity to show my wife the place where I had existed for some time and we had a bite to eat there. Feeling refreshed we then set off on the last mile or so to the work site, through treeland and the inevitable mist.

When we reached the old familiar hacking place it looked as if that, too, was deserted, not a soul to be seen. I called out and the sound of my voice seemed like a rude intrusion on the isolated peace that reigned. Then, like little elves, heads began to appear from behind trees and bushes and the woollen hats they wore added to the image of some pixie like land. Seeing Dorothy put the sappers on their best behaviour and there was no wild reception. It was, however, an occasion for gladness and a chance to forget the drudgery of chopping brushwood. The realisation that they had not been forgotten at this special time glowed in their appreciative eyes and they knew again the joy of their childhood Christmases. My wife and I felt like Santa Claus as we handed out the goodies, and we shall never forget that, without exception, each man gave Dorothy his chocolate ration.

Our visit was a pleasant interlude for the inmates of Acrise Place, and they obviously appreciated us making the trip. There was no end of fuel for the fire and this was soon blazing and heating water for cocoa. We could not stay long because we had to get back to Folkestone Central for a train at 1424 hours and there was the long walk back to the Black Horse Inn and a bus journey to the railway station. We had boosted the morale of the troops somewhat and we set off happily on our return journey.

By the time we reached Folkestone I felt grubby and my boots and gaiters were covered in mud and my battledress crumpled. Standing there on the platform I was aware of two military policemen studying me closely. They could not quite make up their minds about me but the condition of my dress had obviously aroused their suspicions. The strain of doubting became too much for them and I was eventually subjected to their interrogation. 'Where are you going? Where have you come from?' Their arrogance riled me and I told them I was Santa Claus and had been on my rounds. This was spoken light-heartedly but MPs never seem to be free from care or anxiety; gay, merry or cheerful. 'Cut out the comedy,' I was told and with that I shut up and handed them Army form 01735. I am sure they had never before read such an explanation regarding a soldier's journey and they gave me a look of incredibility. It was, at the same time, too mystifying for their brain to fully absorb and the form was returned to me and I continued my journey back to Eastbourne. Dorothy, too, could just as easily have been intercepted in the restricted zone and for this reason she always carried her visitor's permit.

Christmas Day 1942 was a happy time for me; there was the traditional Army good fare served by officers and after having my fill of this I crossed over to 'Sixty' Beach Road and enjoyed the family atmosphere there. Some of my close friends joined us in the evening for fun and games and there was always the Beach Hotel at the corner serving good 'mild' or 'bitter'.

There were dark nights to go with the dark days of war and on occasions such as Christmas there were no brightly lit shops after darkness fell, no Christmas street lights and no Christmas tree bright with coloured lights in sand-bagged town centres. No cheerful Christmas trees decorated with fairy lights shone in house windows when daylight gave way to darkness. There was only blacked out streets and quiet dark countryside, unless the moon shone or the night skies were criss-crossed with searchlights looking for enemy aircraft.

Christmas-time meant trains packed with servicemen and women trying to make it home to spend a precious and all-too-brief Christmas leave with their families. But most people did get out in spite of the blackout and the lack of private transport, and family parties were held. If the moon did not shine then torchlight showed the way to each other's houses, torchlight always directed to the ground with paper to dim the power of a No. 8 battery. Going to parties in the blackout added another dimension to them, especially if everyone was iced with snow and frost and the moon shone.

The food at such parties was very modest with the guests often adding a contribution to the table. But they were great fun and a welcome break in the grey days of war.

The wartime exhortation to 'Post early for Christmas' had then a special urgency unknown today. Christmas parcels, letters and cards, those vital links with home, had to be posted very early to reach the Forces serving in the war zones, and hopefully those who were prisoners of war.

In those days Christmas presents were given in spite of food and clothes rationing, the chronic scarcity of consumer goods in the shops, and repetitive and necessary government calls 'to cut all unnecessary spending'.

As pealing church bells had been chosen in wartime Britain to warn the nation that the country was being invaded it was indeed music to our ears at Eastbourne when it was decreed church bells could once again ring out the joy of that occasion.

Unless one dealt in the 'Black Market' and had good contacts for food, those Christmas cakes, rich with fruit, marzipan and icing, and buttery shortbread, disappeared for the duration of the war. On our festive tables appeared plainer imitations of them. There were a few austerity Christmas puddings available in the shops, and one could have a very modest Christmas lunch in some restaurants. But most housewives, with Christmas coming, tried to put a little from the family rations aside to provide some worthwile fare. A steak pie which represented a few weeks' meat rations, followed by a home-made dumpling type pudding with peel in it. There were not many plump turkeys, chickens or geese around.

Most people celebrated those wartime Christmases as best they could, as did the Forces, when conditions permitted. We wished each other a Merry Christmas and wondered if there would be a peace-time festive season ever again.

There was, however, no respite from the German Luftwaffe and Eastbourne suffered one of its worst bombings about that time. There were heavy casualties near the town centre and 'Bobby's', a big drapery store, dug into their stock of white sheets to cover the dead.

Seaside is a broad thoroughfare, inland from, and about parallel to, the promenade. Dorothy and I, accompanied by Joyce Crossman, with baby Ann in a pram were walking along this street one day when the German hit and run fury was unleashed. Machine gun bullets whizzed all around us and I instinctively threw my body over the child in the pram and sheltered with Joyce against a low wall. In the confusion I did not quite know where Dorothy was but when calm was restored my wife emerged from the protection of a church building. Apart from the shock to her nerves she was rather perturbed by the fact that I had neglected her and our unborn child. Comforting my own would have been the chivalrous thing to do, that is, if one had time to think about it. But in the circumstances in Seaside I reacted differently and can only regret my failure in that instance.

56

Dorothy would have liked to have had the baby in Eastbourne but as things turned out our first born saw the light of day in Edinburgh. Brian was our parents' first grandchild and so excited was my mother that she told my father Dorothy had given birth to a 'beautiful baby boy, nine stone two pounds', instead of nine pounds two ounces.

The pram, with baby inside, soon came to stand outside my parents' ground floor flat home. Dorothy was out attending to Brian one day when Sergeant French, who was home on leave, came along. He made a fuss of the baby but there was a bigger fuss when a captain in Cameronian dress uniform walked out of the house. This was David Mitchell whose mother was a friend of our family and he had been on a visit with her. On seeing one of his former officers, Sergeant French got into a right flutter and did not know which hand to salute with. In the circumstances it would have been sufficient to show respect by standing briefly to attention but Sergeant French's military training dictated otherwise and in his effort to do the right thing he merely became more flustered.

(Bob French returned to Edinburgh after the war and became a postman and I occasionally met him in the Meadowbank area where he lived. At the time of his retirement from the Post Office he was delivering mail in the Dean village area and was very popular there with the residents, so much so that he received a good sum of money to mark the occasion.)

By this time a deep depression had set in with me and I was fed up with 931 Port Construction and Repair Company RE. After all, I was a railway locomotiveman and should have been doing the job I was most suited for. This was my mood when I espied a poster on the wall in our messroom one day. It was all about 'square pegs in round holes' and the Army's concern that every man should be in the right job. I spoke to Lieutenant Robertson about my position and what the poster said and he told me to apply to the OC and have my trade redesignated. I duly acted on his advice and eventually I was sent to Longmoor Camp to be trade tested as a locomotive fireman.

This examination was all over in a day and I returned to Eastbourne. Then came advice that I had been accepted for training as an engine driver at Longmoor and had to proceed there forthwith.

My days with the '931' were over and at this time the command of the company had changed hands. I merely expected to pack my kitbag, say goodbye to my friends and start on a new adventure. But it did not happen like that. I was called to the Company Office where I came face to face with the new OC for the first time.

He invited me to sit down and he said how sorry he was that I was leaving. The '931' needed men like me and there were opportunities for promotion. 'In fact,' he went on, 'I was considering promoting you only the other day.' I had never heard such talk from an officer during the three years I had been in the Army, although Sergeant French had often told McKechnie and me that he could not understand why we did not settle down and join the 'NCOs club'. However, there was no going back now, my mind was made up, and I was looking forward to being a railwayman again. I thanked the OC for his kind consideration, we shook hands, he wished me luck and I was off to the Longmoor Military Railway.

As if to say 'goodbye' the German Luftwaffe turned out in force to see me on my way. I visited Mrs. Tyhurst before leaving Eastbourne and after a chat and the ever welcome 'cuppa' she came to the door with me. Suddenly all hell was let loose as screaming aircraft cast their ominous shadows over the town. The now familiar machine gun fire blended with fierce bomb explosions in an orchestrated symphony of death and Beach Road was shaken to the foundations.

There was no time to seek refuge under the steel table shelter in the sitting room and together Mrs. Tyhurst and I moved under the stairs where she clung to me in trembling fear. I had never seen her in such a state before and I knew then she and Eastbourne could not take much more of the German terror tactics. It was mere chance that I was with her when the Luftwaffe struck and I was glad to be of comfort to that terrified woman.

True to form the enemy disappeared as quickly as he had come and I cautiously opened the door to view the damage. Over on the far side of the road the dust had not yet settled and I did not have to tell Mrs. Tyhurst death had never been so near. Perhaps it was the thought of having survived such a near thing that aided Auntie Ty's recovery, she was soon more or less her old self and we had another cuppa. I had never before said goodbye to a person under such circumstances and I have never experienced a parting like it since.

It may not be obvious at the time but difficult periods in life often turn out to be the best memories. It also seems that we cram more of them into our early years and in later life follow dull routine. For my generation the war years must surely be prominent down memory lane and in my recollections of those times Eastbourne easily comes to mind. The 'sun trap' then was a death trap for many people but the human spirit thrives on adversity and the comradeship spawned is remembered always. I knew as I departed from Beach Road that fateful day I would never forget the experience, and I never have.

INCIDENTS, CASUALTIES AND DAMAGE IN THE BOROUGH

INCIDENTS 1939—1945

Alerts (Red Warning) .... 1350 Incidents 112
      (Local Warning) 861

High Explosive Bombs exploded on or over land 671
  (76 unexploded bombs in addition)
Oil bombs exploded on or over land 28
Incendiary and Phosphorus Incendiary bombs exploded on or
  over land .... approx. 4000
Flying bombs exploded on or over land 15
Shells exploded on or over land 1

Machine and Cannon fire attacks 20
Mines washed ashore
  (13 German, 5 British, 3 unidentified) 21

CASUALTIES

Civilian		Service	
Killed and died in hospital	172	Killed and died in hospital	28
Severely injured	443	Severly injured	63
Slightly injured	489	Slightly injured	92
Missing	2	Missing	-
Total	1106	Total	183

DAMAGE TO PROPERTY

Houses destroyed 475
Houses seriously damaged 1,000
Houses slightly damaged 10,000

ENEMY AIRCRAFT BROUGHT DOWN OR CRASH LANDED IN BOROUGH

Date	Type	Location
16. 8.1940	Hc.111 (believed)	Meads
30. 9.1940	Me.109	Langney
20. 5.1942	Me.109	Downs, near Beachy Head
26. 8.1942	F.W.190	Lottbridge Drove
9.11.1943	Me.410	Friday Street

Information by courtesy of Eastbourne Borough Council
from the publication 'Eastbourne 1939—1945'

Chapter Five

Apart from that brief visit to be trade tested I had never seen Longmoor in my life before. Its existence in Hampshire as a training centre for military railways was also a blind spot in my life. I vaguely recall some awareness of a place other than Derby or Cairnryan where the Royal Engineers were actively engaged in rail transport, but as a young soldier I was more concerned with living and my immediate surroundings rather than the history of the corps and its deployments. As for the men at St. Margaret's who trained at Longmoor every year with the reserves, I hardly knew them and thought not at all of their hobbies.

Longmoor was the first permanent Army camp I had ever seen, and the wooden huts were similar to the First World War surplus units used to house families in Edinburgh in the inter-war years. These were sited outside St. Margaret's where now stands the New Meadowbank sports stadium. The urchins who lived in these huts begged food from the enginemen as they passed to and from work.

The huts at Longmoor were far superior to the hovels in Edinburgh, possibly because they were properly maintained and regularly inspected, and, goodness knows, there was plenty of cheap labour to help preserve them. The roadways, too, were in good condition and there was grass and trees and chain link fencing all enhancing the appearance of the place. The officers' mess, the administration block, the main Naafi and the two-storey barrack blocks were all fine brick buildings but the most impressive structure was undoubtedly St. Martin's Garrison Church.

This church's impressiveness was not so much in its unpretentious brick walls, although these were neat and attractive, it was the interior that had a marked effect on the visitor. Here there was a collection of memorials to the men of the Transportation Services who fell in World War One and these have since been added to in recognition of the sacrifices in World War Two. The origins of the church are humble— until 1931 it was a forage barn, but in that year the first work of the conversion was completed.

In addition to self help by the garrison troops, an unexpected windfall in the form of the Garden-Fund raised by the troops who ran allotments during World War One came to light in a Petersfield bank. This was used to commission the reredos designed by the late Martin Travers and dedicated in April 1936.

This striking work of the risen Christ aroused much interest and soon more ambitious plans were being formed and the four main line railway companies and the London Passenger Transport Board were asked to support by donating stained glass windows to commemorate their men who had fallen in World War One. Their response was spontaneous and generous and resulted in five beautiful windows, again the work of Martin Travers. Each window contains the patron saints of the two cathedrals or countries associated with the donor railway, together with the coats of arms and boroughs associated with the railway systems. These patron saints are:

GWR St. David (Wales) and St. George (England).
LMSR St. Mungo (Glasgow) and St. Alban (St. Albans).
LNER St. Andrew (Scotland) and St. Peter (York).
SR St. Mary (Salisbury) and St. Augustine (Canterbury).
LPTB St. Edward the Confessor (Westminster) and St. Paul (City of London).

After World War Two further windows following the same general principles in design were added. These windows contain only one saint, the lower half of the window being filled with an appropriate coat of arms or symbols of the donors. The saints portrayed in these windows are:

Canadian National and Pacific Railways—St. Lawrence.
Port of London Authority—St. Nicholas (patron saint of sailors).
Transportation and Movement Control—St. Christopher (patron saint of travellers).

After the death of Mr. Travers his work was continued by Lawrence Lee who maintained a great interest in the church. Three further windows have now been presented. The first, presented by the Inland Water Transport Old Comrades to commemorate those who fell in World War Two depicts St. Martin, the patron saint of the church. The second is a rose window incorporating the coat of arms of the Royal Engineers, presented by regular serving and retired sapper officers. The final window was presented jointly by the Royal Engineers and the Royal Army Service Corps as an inspiration to the Royal Corps of Transport on its formation in 1965. This window portrays St. James the Great, a valiant Christian soldier who became a legend closely associated with transport by land and sea.

In addition to these memorial windows there are a number of memorial plaques. Some commemorate the service of the Supplementary Reserve railway units. Two of note are the bronze tablets to the memory of officers and men of the 755th and 763rd Railway Shop Battalions of the United States Army Transportation Corps. Finally there are two tablets commemorating people closely associated with Longmoor and its church. One is to John Aiton Kay, formerly editor of the Railway Gazette who did much to encourage the work of the Royal Engineers Transportation Service and to stimulate interest in the church and its memorials. The latest tablet, unveiled on Remembrance Day 1972, is to the memory of Lieutenant Colonel Ernest Woodhouse, that dedicated railwayman and benefactor of Longmoor church and garrison.

Although the church cannot claim to be an outstanding example of ecclesiastical architecture, there can be few collections of modern stained glass windows equal to the memorial windows and none with such unique associations. In all there are over 100 crests and coats of arms presented in this notable heraldic display. The linking of saints with military and technical services is of interest to soldier, civilian, artist and layman alike.

After the closure of Longmoor in 1969 there was limited activity there involving Units of the Royal Corps of Transport but eventually in 1977 Longmoor and Borden camps ceased to exist and the remnants of a great enterprise were transferred to Leconfield, North Humberside. St. Martin's Garrison Church also went to Leconfield and there on June 1st, 1978 there was an inaugural service to mark the continuance of a great spiritual tradition that is so much a part of the Corps of Royal Engineers.

The main parade ground was the heart of Longmoor camp and like the human heart was not quite in the middle of the co-ordinated body. The Longmoor body was known as the No. 1 Railway Training Centre RE which, in September 1942, became the Transportation Training Centre to reflect a new and wider role.

Facing the main parade ground was the headquarters building which was well styled in brick and of even proportions. Here were the offices for the staff, a telephone exchange, a conference room and drawing offices used both for the preparation of drawings for the construction of the railway and also for training draughtsmen and surveyors in railway trades. In my time at Longmoor there was a sentry at the main entrance to this headquarters and many a wearisome two hours I have spent looking out over the sleeping camp.

Directly across the parade ground from the headquarters block there was the Regimental Police post fronted by white-washed posts and fencing and nice red fire buckets. This is where men on jankers reported for their extra duties while confined to camp. This is where one heard the call, 'Get your hands out of your pockets!' or, 'Fasten up your tunic sapper!' These fault spotters who wore armbands with the initials 'RP' also expected passing soldiers to salute the empty parade ground, which was the traditional means of showing respect for the corps.

I remember one evening when I was encompassing the parade ground (one never walked across it, apart from drilling there) I met the Commandant, Brigadier H.A. Joly de Lotbiniere MC. We two were alone on the road and I decided a man with all that red tape on his hat and shoulders warranted a very smart salute. I was no stranger to the art of saluting on the march with head turned towards the officer and I felt I excelled myself with the Brigadier. How surprised I was when he beckoned me over. 'Sapper,' he said, 'fasten up your neck, the RP's in this camp are proper b's,' and in a hushed tone he told me what he meant by 'b's'.

Slightly north west of the headquarters block and adjacent to the main road there was the Kitchener Theatre. This large building was used for shows and other entertainment or mass meetings. It was at a gathering in the Kitchener Theatre that I first heard a speaker addressing the audience as, 'Gentlemen of the Royal Engineers and men of other regiments.'

St. Martin's Church was a short distance to the west of the Kitchener Theatre with the guardroom interposing. All these buildings were near the main Liphook road. Across the road to the north was Longmoor Station and signalbox which were nearly, but not quite, the half way mark on the eight mile stretch of railway between Liss and Bordon. Weavers Down and Liss Forest Road were the intermediate stations between Longmoor and Liss and between Longmoor and Bordon there were Woolmer, Whitehill and Oakhanger. There was also a loop line between Longmoor and Whitehill known as the Hollywater Line. The intermediate stations were Griggs Green, Holm Hills and Hollywater and the length four miles.

The railway was what Longmoor was all about and to the east of the station there was a large complex of railway buildings and sidings. Here was the locomotive shed, carriage shed, signal school, offices, workshops and the classroom where potential engine drivers were put through their paces. It was three weeks of theory in the school and five weeks out on the line for practical training, a total of eight weeks. Not far away, on higher ground was Weavers Down where the field work training was carried out. If the wind was blowing the wrong way while gas drill was being carried out at Weavers Down it could be an unpleasant experience for men working in the railway yard.

I commenced my eight-week course on 17th May 1943 and at that time QMSI Tom Weavings was in charge of the school. I was to meet him years

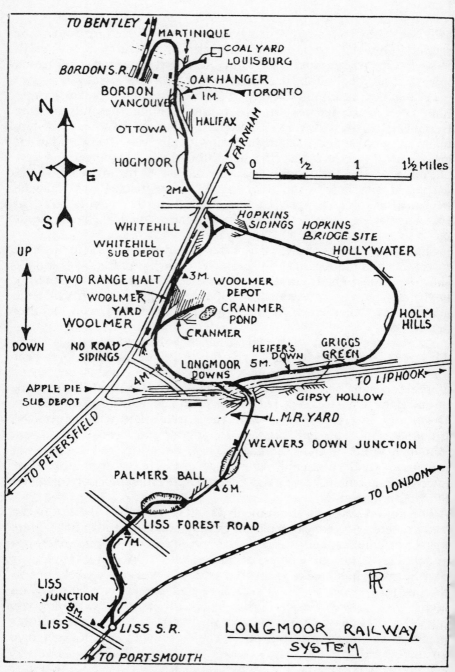

Longmoor Railway System Map courtesy of R. Tourret from 'War Department Locomotives'.

later about two o'clock in the morning at Skipton Station. He was, by then, a locomotive inspector with British Railways and had turned out for the passage of a train taking Princess Margaret to Scotland. I had to introduce myself after so many years, but our ex 'schoolmaster' was pleased to see me. Apart from anything else he could not be expected to remember every trainee that passed through the school, there must have been hundreds. What I remember about him most at Longmoor was his mood some mornings when he had 'a liver on' as they used to say. At such times the QMSI used to stay in his office.

There were two sergeant instructors who specialised in particular subjects, but nevertheless had an overall knowledge of the steam locomotive and rules and regulations. We were issued with note books and the Military Railway Rule Book which had been brought up to date in 1938. The rule book, like a soldier's pay book, was a personal item and had to be carried while on duty.

The course was a comprehensive one and we learned the rules and the steam locomotive thoroughly. The instructors prided themselves in being able to quote any rule completely and certain things about the locomotive lent themselves to memorising, such as the five positions and events of the Westinghouse air brake, the passage of steam from the boiler and the port openings in the cylinders at particular crank settings. There were, of course, the inevitable jokes to ease the strain of learning, usually after a serious session had ended. 'What would you do to avoid black smoke?' Answer, 'Whitewash the coal.' 'Why is the dome situated on top of the boiler?' Answer, 'To make the engine look tippy.'

Although instruction was available on the LNER and other railways it was organised by the men themselves and not by the company. Those old companies would hardly provide accommodation and certainly not tuition. So, it was a nice change to see the Army so well organised. Not only were locomotivemen being trained, there were courses available for every conceivable railway and fieldwork trade and at one time in 1943 there were 900 men going through their paces. In all, Longmoor trained 76,000 men during the war years. The peak strength of Longmoor garrison reached 7000 permanent staff whilst the turnover of personnel exceeded 27,000.

With so many men being trained it is not surprising that the instructors had to deal with all kinds of people. Sergeant Kenneth Stokes was an instructor I greatly admired. He had that unique talent of creating interest and imparting information in such a way that the student did not easily forget what he had been told. Sergeant Stokes was always very smart in appearance and fully conversant with every aspect of railway operation. He was brimful of confidence and this self reliance was transmitted to others through his pleasing personality. He was indeed an asset to the permanent staff at Longmoor and as the hundreds of trainees became qualified in their respective fields they took with them to many war fronts the knowledge and confidence imparted by Sergeant Kenneth Stokes.

With the cessation of hostilities he took up his former employment with the London Midland Region of British Railways, where his instructional ability again proved most useful, as he passed on to others his wide knowledge of oil burning steam locomotives and diesels. He became a running foreman and a locomotive inspector but always his first love was imparting knowledge and improving the efficiency of locomotivemen. Kenneth now lives in semi-retirement at Sheffield (he teaches music) but he has never forgotten Longmoor and the many sappers he helped on their way. He remembers, too, some of the more unusual instances during his sojourn at the LMR school.

'Kitchener', a tank engine, was converted to oil burning—a most unsuitable choice, incidentally. A lance corporal driver and sapper fireman parked this loco in a siding opposite Longmoor Down Station and went for a Naafi break. During their absence the oil burner valve leaked oil into the firepan and blazing oil ran onto the ground. When the crew returned the sleepers and wooden rail keys were burned away and 'Kitchener' was settled comfortably on Mother Earth.

QSMI Tom Weavings was conducting initial interviews when a brash sapper went into the Loco School Office. 'Railway experience?' Tom asked. 'Great Western; six months cleaner, six months fireman; and when called up, six months driver,' said the sapper.

Tom gave him his well known quizzical look and shouted to Kenneth in the next room, 'A case of rapid promotion here Sergeant Stokes—18 months service on the Great Western and now a driver.'

Kenneth, who was also conducting interviews, interrupted his work and asked the cheeky sapper the rates of pay he had been on. Other than the cleaning rate the 'get there quickly' lad had not a clue and he soon realised that the soldier instructors were fully alert to the situation in Civvy Street. The Smart Aleck was duly put down for a fireman's course.

Corporal Fiske, on the permanent staff, had been on the Great Western Railway—he said, as a driver. Being in his forties he may well have been. However, one dark night in the blackout he arrived at Liss, ran round his train, coupled up again and on receiving a green lamp opened the regulator. Alas, he had omitted to reverse his engine and so moved smoothly towards the stop block and it was only when the rear coach was deposited right on top of the block that poor old Fiske realised his mistake.

Sergeant Stokes eventually succeeded Tom Weavings as WO in charge of School Interviews. A fair haired sapper formerly a fireman at Heaton shed, informed Kenneth that he had just come out of the Glass House (Detention Centre) and had long been without leave. He said that he had no intention of trying to pass the course though he said he was very interested in railway work.

Kenneth went to see the OC of 'P' Company and told him about the sapper and suggested that he be granted privilege leave and then be included in the next course. The OC agreed and Kenneth went back to the school and informed the sapper of the decision at which he was overjoyed, saying that he would really get dug into the course on his return from leave. He did not return.

Months afterwards Kenneth was in the WO and Sergeants Mess one evening and a young sergeant came up to him and told him he had been Court Martial Orderly Sergeant that day at Woolmer Camp.

The Convening Officer had been Major Sir Geoffrey Palmer, Bart. Coldstream Guards and the 'wandering sapper' had been on charge. After the evidence had been presented Sir Geoffrey asked the sapper if he had anything to say before he was sentenced. 'Yes,' replied the deserter, 'I think that you are a fornicated old bastard.' And he never even said 'Sir'!

John was a corporal, soon to be promoted sergeant. A Premium Apprentice on the LNER he was a tall, smart chap with extensive theoretical knowledge. At the outbreak of war he had been Running Foreman, at Helensburgh.

Everyone in the Loco Department at Longmoor had to do two months of practical work as a driver or fireman. John was doing his driving stint and it came to pass that he was working the 2215 Liss to Longmoor one dark Sunday night. This was a most unpopular train to work, crammed full of roistering soldiery full of local ale and the air resounded to voices raised in song punctuated by occasional screams from ATS girls misguided enough to be passengers in the dark coaches.

John stopped at Liss Forest Road and the loco would not start the train up the bank. So, John reversed and set back to get a thrust at the train. However, while John's train had been stopped, the Liss Forest Road being a passing point on the single line, the 2200 passenger train from Longmoor to Liss had moved away from Liss Forest Road en route to Liss and John's rear coach collided with the centre of the 2200 ex Longmoor.

The sappers' choir changed their tune and screams and shouts rent the air. Speed had been low and apart from shock there were no injuries but what a job it proved to be for the breakdown gang! John was reduced to the rank of sapper but ere long he got his three stripes and finished up in the 21st Army Group in France.

The most fantastic railway accident of all time! Before it occurred breakdown crews were being alerted and the Duty Officer was on his way to the scene. This is how it happened.

On Friday night the sappers stayed in camp bulling up for Saturday morning military training and saving their coppers for Saturday night visits to the high life of Petersfield (?). The 2245 Bordon to Longmoor stopped at Oakhanger and, on receiving the 'right away', started again. But, prior to the arrival of the passenger train the Blockman at Oakhanger had allowed a freight train out of the sidings en route to Bordon and he forgot to reverse the points. Instead of proceeding on the main line the passenger train turned into the sidings and ran towards a huge concrete stop block. Modern interlocking would have made this impossible but, apart from the expense, military railways did not easily lend themselves to this sophisticated equipment.

The blackout was so complete that the driver and fireman and trainee fireman did not realise where exactly they were. The horror-struck Blockman realised his error when he saw the train's tail lamp turn into Toronto Sidings and he immediately rang Control.

The Controller, a sergeant who had formerly been an LNER signalman rang the Loco Depot at Longmoor where 'Dixie' Dean was the Running Foreman on duty. 'Dixie,' he said, 'get the breakdown men out, we are going to have a smash!' Dixie sent out shed staff for the breakdown crew and the Duty Officer set out.

Fortunately there were four wagons loaded with ashes against the stop block and the Southern Railway tankie smashed them up so completely that a Southern Freight Rolling Stock Inspector said he found it impossible to get the wagon numbers.

After the dust had settled the driver rubbed his bruises and went back to see how the passengers and guard had fared. There was only one passenger, a Canadian, who was drunk. This worthy leaned out of the carriage window and said, 'Don't forget to stop at Whitehill.' He apparently thought that what had just taken place was a normal LMR stop.

RMS Dimmock at Longmoor had been in the Corps for donkey's years, in fact, it was rumoured he was once on a charge for having a dirty bow and arrow! Passing the Barrack Square, where prominent notices warned it was out of bounds when not on parade, the RSM saw a sapper in the middle of the Square, hands in pockets, Woodbine between lips, surveying the ornate Administration Block. 'Dimm' could not believe his eyes and incoherent with rage he went up to the sapper. This worthy looked at Dimm and chattily remarked, 'I tell you what, Mate, your place would make a bloody fine Working Men's Club.'

Kenneth was in the Loco School Office marking exam papers when there was a knock at the door and in response to the instructor's 'Enter' there appeared the strangest sapper he had ever seen. He was about

5 years of age, snow white hair, smart bearing, three 1914—18 ribbons and, surprise-surprise, the purple and white ribbon of the Military Cross, thus proving Commissioned Rank.

Somehow his face was vaguely familiar so Kenneth sent him to the back door of the nearby Naafi for tea and wads for both of them. A gunner officer, the visitor had been recalled in September 1939 and, strangely, had been quickly 'bowler hatted'. After a short spell in industry which he could not stick he volunteered, like the man in the poem, as a 'Private in the Buffs'.

Having some railway experience he had been transferred to the Royal Engineers and found himself at the TT Wing at Longmoor. On reporting to RSM McAusland at the Loco Depot he was sent up to the Loco School to 'make himself useful'. Kenneth soon realised who he was, he had been Assistant District Motive Power Superintendent at Holbeck, Leeds when Kenneth started there in 1924 but soon departed under a cloud.

In the Army the 'powers that be' looked after him and although he had to do his stint as a driver- incidentally scaring stiff all the firemen by his erratic driving allied with poor eyesight—he soon became a sergeant and was made a Running Foreman. There was no separate bunk for him so he applied to live out.

He went to stay at the Area Naafi Manager's home, this gentleman having been an Indian Army captain so the two were well matched. The captain's wife was a real good looker—she had at one time been an actress and was very much younger than her husband. She must have preferred older men for when the RE sergeant (ex Major) was demobilised with group one he departed and took along with him the glamorous wife, although it transpired she was not a 'wife' at all!

Six Polish soldiers had to be trained as railway saboteurs, along with a British sergeant of the Parachute Regiment. They were to be dropped in enemy occupied territory with the object of wrecking loco sheds. For this purpose they had to be trained on how to move a loco and various ways and methods of damage, for example, plastic explosive on clack boxes, damage to firebox etc.

Sergeant Stokes took out a Southern 0-6-0 tender loco which had a fairly roomy footplate. Regulations as to number of men allowed on the footplate, i.e. four, were shelved. The fireman on this occasion was from Gateshead.

They trundled their way round the Hollywater Loop, each in turn having a go at driving. At Griggs Green they stabled and ate their packed lunches. It was a lovely day and Kenneth and his mate were treated to a demonstration of their companions' toughness with a display of unarmed combat. Soon it was time to return to the shed. Kenneth stood at the front of the tender while the trainees and fireman occupied the cab.

As they crossed the main Liphook road approaching the run down to the coal stage there was one almighty bang—a gauge glass had burst and the party was engulfed in hot water and steam. There was panic and all but Kenneth baled out with the fireman leading the way. This allowed Kenneth to get to the steam and water cocks and shut same and apply the brake and await the return of his jittery gang.

His first well chosen words were addressed to the fireman then a few to the remainder. 'Sorry, Sarge,' someone said, 'we thought the bloody thing was going to blow up.'

Kenneth stopped the loco just before reaching the coal stage, telling the trainess of the limited clearance and to keep their heads in. As they moved towards the shute one of them stuck his head out whereupon the instructor yelled, 'Look out you bloody fool.' Fortunately the Pole came to no harm but he remarked pensively, 'Zee Sergeant he say look out you bloody fool and what he mean was look in—ah zis English!'

Apart from these amusing incidents which could be multiplied a thousand times there were also 'howlers' in the exam papers Kenneth marked, mostly firemen's papers.

Situated above the boiler is the Rams Bottom Valve Gear.

Four blasts on a shunters whistle means ease couplinks.

Water gauges are provided for the prevention of fireboxes.

Steam goes to the lubricator which then turns to water.

It is dangerous to carry water in the boiler because the engine will start to prime.

The safety valve is fitted to stop the engine from blowing off.

The steam jet creates a good impression with the fire.

I would increase the supply of secondary air by opening the smokebox door.

Steam passes into the eternal steam pipe.

Air passes the Artillary Reservoir.

I would sign on and repent to the foreman.

Green handsignal from platelayer means proceed at danger.

Before protecting train the fireman must get the driver's insurance.

Steam goes to atmosphere via the blasted pipe.

A Wrong Line Order is a verbal instruction in writing.

Fire less and more often and so keep a well burning bright fire thereof.

The smokebox door must be tightly closed, if not, it might fall off and hit someone walking on the railway.

The fireman must read all notices and then sing on in the presence of the foreman.

Our sleeping accommodation was spacious and we used double bunks. The quarters were inspected every morning and beds and kits had to be made up and in order. The only exceptions were people who were on night duty and these men were usually well covered during the inspection. This did not prevent the sergeant major having a look at them and he would sometimes pull the blankets back and ask the sleeper if he wanted to buy a battleship?' This is the kind of incident that gave Longmoor Camp a touch of humaneness and relieved the sombreness of a moorland setting.

The importance of keeping fit was never overlooked and it was 'everybody out' and onto the parade ground for half an hour's physical training before breakfast. We had to dress in PT kit and the exercises were less than strenuous, but it is surprising the number of men who hid in the toilets and elsewhere to avoid 'limbering up'. There was no roll call on the parade ground but NCO's visited the men's quarters and anyone found there had to have a good excuse. It was quite a sight to see hundreds of men in vest and pants moving gymnastically to a single command. The exercise gave one a good appetite for breakfast and one felt all the better for it.

The mess halls were clean and well ventilated and the food adequate and well cooked. Like all army cookhouses there was extra labour available for chores like cleaning and preparing vegetables. Being an established camp Longmoor had its quota of ATS and these girls worked as cooks and on clerical work. They had their own quarters in the west side of the camp and this area was strictly out of bounds to all male personnel.

On pay parade we used to form up in three ranks waiting for the pay out to be organised. The ATS were involved in this along with the pay officer. While we were waiting, our little sergeant major would be pacing up and down criticising our appearance and conduct and obviously happy to have a captive audience. One of his criticisms was men swearing within earshot of the girls. He stood facing us with his back to the office and unknown to him two ATS girls were at the door. There he was laying it on about swearing and unconsciously using an oath every few words to emphasise his meaning. The girls were looking over to us and shaking their heads in mock despair.

Apart from the usual sports and the camp cinema there was not much in the way of recreation at Longmoor. To meet the civilian population one had to travel to Petersfield, the nearest large town, about six miles from Liss. There was also Bordon, a smaller place, but more convenient for travel. Whatever direction one took the LMR was the usual mode of transport. There was much hilarity on the last train from Liss on a Saturday night, there being no lights in the carriages and a journey over dark moorland. The only relief to the pitch blackness was the glow from the locomotive fire, which could not be completely hidden by blackout sheets, and when passengers struck a match or shone a torch there was momentary illumination. Most of the time we were in darkness, with perhaps the glow from a cigarette to mark a person's position in the compartment.

As in the First World War there was a large contingent of Canadian forces at Bordon. These men were better dressed and better paid and this could cause some resentment amongst British troops. There was little to worry about in the isolation of Longmoor, but if one ventured to Bordon and farther afield to Aldershot where French Canadians were in force there could be trouble brewing. Sometimes, of course, there were riots for no real reason at all when men became frustrated and very drunk, then damage to property and the hurting of people would ensue and the police, military and civilian, would be very busy.

While I was at school I was free at the weekends, apart from the church parade on Sunday. When practical training began, however, there was shift work and a real chance of being on duty on Saturday. Sergeant Major McAusland, an ex Glasgow (Parkhead) engine driver, was in charge of the engine shed and was the equivalent of locomotive foreman, or shedmaster, as the position was later known.

On the footplate a trainee was watched over by an NCO while the locomotive was in the care of a driver and fireman on the permanent staff, or the Depot Wing, as it was officially known. What we had learned so diligently in the classroom had now to be put into practice.

I was no stranger to the rudiments of engine driving and in Edinburgh I had driven many different types, but always under the supervision of a driver who, in the end, was the man responsible for the performance and condition of the locomotive. Now, I was the driver and the engine and the fireman were my responsibility. I was left in no doubt of this by the instructor and we had been well told about it at school.

When a man signed on duty it was an indication that he had read and understood the notices posted.

Sometimes I joined the engine at the shed and on other occasions I was told to travel on a particular service for instruction. The latter was to be preferred because there was all the preparation work to be done at the shed, a dirty job at any time. This, however, was an essential part of training and helped one to understand the mechanics of a locomotive so much more. It was also an opportunity to see any defects before going into service and the onus was on the trainee to spot defects and report same for attention. The regular driver and instructor stood aside and did not interfere, although they were vigilant and ready for the worst.

The important thing is to familiarise oneself with the particular locomotive, since no two are alike. One must get the feel of the steam regulator and determine the amount of opening necessary before steam gets to work in the cylinders. Anyone can start a steam engine but stopping it is a different matter. It is important therefore that a driver knows the efficiency or otherwise of the brake. Then he must ensure he has sufficient fuel and water for the task ahead and that all the necessary tools are available and properly stacked. The fireman is there to do much of this but it is the driver's overall responsibility. Last, but not least, the driver checks that he has his rule book with him. This is a requirement on all railways but on the LMR where the rules and method of signalling was a little different it was a comfort to feel the rule book in one's pocket.

The theoretical and practical instruction can be learned and committed to memory but only experience can put the shine on a driver's performance. Some people are so heavy handed that they will go on making fierce brake applications throughout their railway careers and passengers, guards and goods all suffer as a result. There is a definite technique to be adopted, particularly with the Westinghouse air brake, a very powerful brake. Only practice and care can ensure good braking and, thankfully, most engine drivers develop the right technique and provide a smooth journey.

As if to frustrate learner drivers there are also signals to learn and line gradients, one must know where to apply steam and where to reduce the supply to the cylinders or cut it off completely. There is also the braking power to consider consistent with the weight of the train, to say nothing of the need to watch cab gauges and the fireman. To add to the difficulties at Longmoor there was the blackout and a strange mode of signalling.

In general, military railway signalling followed British Railway practice although distant signals are not always used. Improvised flagboard signalling was developed at Longmoor for use in war conditions. Its merit was its undoubted simplicity and the fact that the signals could quickly be improvised from salvaged material.

The use of the flagboard signalling on the LMR was extensive and a necessity for trainees destined for the various theatres of war. In the military flagboard signalling system the outer home signal is called the Station Limit Board and shows on the section side a black diamond on a white background and on the station side the letters 'SL' also in black and white. The board measures approximately three feet square.

The home signal is known as the flagboard and measures approximately four feet six inches by three feet. On this can be hung flags, painted boards or metal plates or, at night, lamps. The upper portion of the board shows the aspect of the home signal whilst the lower portion indicates the aspect of the outer home. The starting signal is given by the Blockman showing a green hand signal from the box.

If a distant signal is required a Warning Board is used, taking the form of a large slatted white board (about ten feet by eight feet). The virtue of these military signals lies in the ease with which they could be made up. Add to this a field telephone and one is in the railway business.

The first locomotive I drove at Longmoor was Kitchener (2), a side tank engine with 0-6-2 wheel arrangement. This engine was delivered to Longmoor in 1938 and was the first for 16 years. It was essentially an instructional locomotive and was fitted with both Westinghouse and vacuum brakes as well as Lambert wet sanding gear. Stone's electric generator and lights were fitted also as these had been found most successful on earlier locomotives.

Although designed for coal burning this locomotive was converted to oil burning (again for instructional purposes) in July 1942. When I climbed aboard Kitchener (2) at Longmoor Station the noise from the fierce fire was tantamount to the jet-like whine of a great blow lamp trapped in the close confines of the engine cab. It was a passenger train with about two coaches and on seeing me the driver immediately retired to a compartment leaving me with the instructor and fireman.

The whole journey from Liss to Bordon took about half an hour with stops at all stations; so my first effort would last about 15 minutes. From Longmoor to Woolmer there was a slightly falling gradient on a right hand curve and with the advantage of a light train it was opportune to get the feel of the brake. Over on the left there was Applepie Depot, a stores compound made famous in the song, 'Hurrah for the CRE'.

It was double line working from Longmoor to Woolmer with the usual semaphore signals. Between Woolmer and Oakhanger there were tablets to exchange on the single line and from Oakhanger to Bordon a staff was in use on the single line. Without going into any technical details these tablets and staff were tangible authority from the signalman to the driver to occupy the single line and on these were inscribed the station names.

The fireman was competent in dealing with the exchange of tokens but the instructor was watchful that I, as the driver, made sure the respective tokens applied to the line we were to run on. So, my concentration on driving was disturbed when I did the necessary to satisfy the instructor. Between Woolmer and Bordon the semaphore signals gave way to Station Limit Boards and Flagboards and braking distances were marked by the large slatted white boards suitably placed in fields near the lineside.

Apart from learning the route I was getting to know the locations where some of my barrack room friends worked as blockmen and seeing them helped to ease the tension of driving with an instructor breathing down my neck. Not that he interfered unduly, but no one likes to be watched all the time and I was no exception. So it was with some relief that the day came when I was on my own in full charge.

At the age of 23 I was far removed from the engine driver image of fresh cheeks, rubber collar and white hair, and there was no trace of portliness. Sometimes my fireman was old enough to be my father and had the experience to match but lacked, however, the confidence to succeed as a driver.

At the outbreak of war in 1939 there were six steam engines in service on the LMR and three derelict. Of those in service Sir John French, Selborne and Kitchener were reliable and in good order. Earl Roberts was available, but not up to the increasing demands, whilst Gordon and Marlborough were not fit for heavy work. Kingsley, Earl Haig and Wellington were out of use.

Additional motive power was urgently required, both to handle the increased traffic of troops and stores and to cater for the large scale training programmes which were starting. The only solution was to requisition, borrow or buy, locomotives from the main line companies. It was not surprising, therefore, that the line up at Longmoor Shed in 1943 was a mixture of WD engines and some formerly owned by the four main line railway companies. The LNER was well represented with a group of J68/J69 0-6-0 tank engines with Westinghouse brakes fitted for the Liverpool Street suburban services. There were no familiar North British locomotives as there had been in the first war, but all steam engines are basically alike and differ only in design and capability. The original Army engines were marked LMR with a name above while the newcomers had the former company lettering and number painted out and marked WD with a new number.

Most of these engines were well worn and performed indifferently but when I first took my turn at yard shunting I made the acquaintance of a completely new engine. This was the WD Austerity with an 0-6-0 wheel arrangement and a saddle tank and built by Hunslet at Leeds. It was not a handsome engine but was squat and seemed over-burdened like an Army mule. The steam actuated parts were out of sight within the framing and only the coupling rods, which distributed the power over the six wheels, could be readily seen.

When under steam there was a distinctive bark from the exhaust, a faculty which seemed to speak its potential capacity. In contrast to other locomotives there seemed less delay in the passage of steam from the dome to the cylinders and one felt that the steam was actually stored in the cylinders and on tap.

With a wheel base of 11 feet this compared favourably with Kitchener's 7 feet when it came to pushing in clear in a siding. The wee Austerity's tractive effort was also in excess of anything the Army had had previously. Add to this light axle load of 16½ tons and one can appreciate there were advantages in its simplicity.

These engines along with their larger austere stablemates were produced in large numbers for the impending invasion of Europe. They were required to deal with the build up of traffic in Britain as well as the follow up, once a foothold had been gained abroad. When the decision to build these locomotives had been made, the North British Locomotive Company in Glasgow suspended all work on armaments and went over entirely to the production of large tender Austerities. The mobility of warfare determined that the highest priority should be given to locomotives and orders from the Ministry of Supply were received for freight locomotives of LMS 2-8-0 design suitably modified for service in various theatres of war. The first of these was delivered in July 1940 and in due course a total of 133 were in service.

The 'Austerity WD' locomotive of 2-8-0 arrangement was ordered by the Ministry of Supply in 1942. Drawings were prepared and materials ordered 16 days after the placing of the order and within five months the first of 545 units was delivered. A 2-10-0 type was also placed in service five months after work in the drawing ofice had commenced and 150 were delivered. As a counter to aerial cannon fire an experiemental armoured engine was built to the specifications of the War Office and, in order to comply with the rigid weight limitations, an ingenious means of attaching the armour was devised.

In all, 1200 locomotives of a wide variety were supplied by the NBL Company, together with an impressive quantity of spare boilers and other parts.

The Vulcan foundry in Lancashire was similarly engaged in building these engines but to a lesser extent. America also produced their equivalent to the British Austerity and during my time in the Army I was eventually to sample them all, some coal burners and some oil burners. But it was Germany, with control over all Europe, who really mass-produced the Austerity locomotives and during the war years thousands were built in Germany and occupied countries.

Like the liberty boats being built in America the expected life span of these Austerity engines was about three years, but with the cessation of hostilities they were widely used throughout Britain and Europe. In the post war years St. Margaret's used quite a number of the 2-8-0's on heavy freight trains and they were hauling coal from Fife to Aberdeen right up to 1969 and the demise of steam on British Railways. The LNER alone bought 75 of the 0-6-0 saddle tanks before nationalisation and they were popular for shunting duties. The NCB also realised the value of these little engines and used them widely in collieries.

Long after I had departed from Longmoor the wee Austerities became the backbone of the LMR stud. Some wore out and were supplemented by others but one named Brussels was rebuilt by Hunslet in 1958 to WD

War Standard Specification incorporating numerous improvements which included oil firing, Westinghouse brakes and such details as safety footsteps for shunters! Thus modified, Brussels ran until January 1969 when the Brussels Preservation Society purchased it. After a spell in storage this locomotive found a home in Yorkshire with the Keighley and Worth Valley Light Railway at Haworth. Instead of the three years expected of them some of these engines have surpassed the designers greatest expectations, and I little thought that when I drove one of the first of their kind in 1943 I would still be seeing them in preservation yards throughout Britain in the late seventies.

As my training progressed at Longmoor I became more confident and felt I knew the locomotives and the railway they ran on, including the signals. One Saturday afternoon I went engine and van from Longmoor to Bordon to work back a slack coupled train of heavy rails. After shunting the train to the platform line at Bordon the Blockman gave me a key token that authorised my passage to Longmoor. Being a Saturday the intermediate boxes were switched out.

Just before departure a Canadian ATS girl came along and asked if she and her friends could get a lift to Longmoor. I referred her to the guard who was already in the only suitable vehicle on the train for passengers, and looking back I could see a group of Canadian females beside the brakevan. Could be the guard had told the girl to ask the driver but I immediately 'put the ball back to him'.

On receiving the signal to proceed from the Blockman I looked back for a wave from the guard and this was immediate. I also noticed the girls were standing on the brakevan verandah. The load was heavy and the engine was labouring to get it under way. Once on the move the train continued to increase speed and I anticipated a clear run to Longmoor.

It was a lovely afternoon and as I expected the signals were all in my favour. Approaching Woolmer the semaphore distant signal was 'off' and I thought, that's me right through to Longmoor. Being a slack coupled train I only had use of the engine brake and there was the guard's handbrake, if required. This, along with a rising gradient approaching Longmoor was ample stopping power as far as I was concerned.

When I caught sight of the Home signal opposite Woolmer blockpost, I was amazed to see the signal arm jerking up and down. 'What's this in aid of?' I said to my mate, but he was as surprised as I was to witness something so unusual. Being uncertain of the situation I decided to stop and find out what all the wagging was about.

Mindful of the heavy train I had behind me I could not just slap on the brake and grind to a halt. I operated the brake handle like a see-saw, gradually gathering up the weight of the train and feeling it push against the engine buffers. At the same time I was watching the Home signal and

77

its waving arm. Before long I was past the signal and the engine wheels stopped turning. When I looked back there was a space of about a dozen wagons between the engine and the train and I could see the brake van in the distance with all the girls waving.

It was obviously a case of 'accidental division' as the railway terms it and I was relieved that the accident had happened on level ground. I had reversed the engine and was moving back to investigate the trouble when the blockman climbed aboard. 'What's the idea of wagging that signal in my face?' I said. 'Oh,' he replied, 'I wanted you to stop to give me a lift into Longmoor.' I was lost for words as I climbed down to see what had caused the breakaway.

Hanging on the drawhook of the vehicle next to the engine was a broken three link coupling, which should never have been used in the first place. They are much lighter than locomotive couplings and more convenient to hook on with a shunting pole. But on seeing the mess we were in the guard realised that convenience should not always be the first consideration and with such a heavy train there should have been no hesitation in using the engine coupling.

I realised I had to move fast, before a search party was sent out to look for us and I immediately removed the broken coupling and buried it at the side of the line. I then put on the engine coupling and got underway again as the guard returned to his van. Having seen all the trouble he had caused the blockman remained silent and I concentrated on getting to Longmoor Yard as quickly as possible.

As expected the blockman at Longmoor was at the window shouting down, 'Where have you been?' I rubbed my hands together in a gesture of being cold and pointed to the engine. This was, on occasions, the true reason for losing time but there were no steaming difficulties that day. The alternative to blaming the engine would have been a long report on what had actually happened and, being Saturday afternoon, I was more concerned about getting finished.

The code of safety on British Railways is stricter than that of military railways, for obvious reasons. Men being trained at Longmoor were likely to be operating some kind of railway service far removed from the long established main lines in Britain. In war, railways were a prime target and we were liable to be bombed and sabotaged. It was the sappers' job to get these lines operational as quickly as possible and there was no time to stand on ceremony and follow the more stringent rules. In these cirumstances reasonable chances had to be taken but in an organised way.

Part of the training syllabus at Longmoor took account of active service conditions when there would be no mechanical or electrical safety devices incorporated in the signalling system. Emergency methods of working such as time interval, line clear message and ticket and permissive block were used more freely than in civilian practice. Safe working depended on common sense and strict telephone discipline. The emphasis was on keeping traffic moving rather than the strictest standards of safety. When this is considered against the background of the military need, the possibility of enemy interference and the lower speeds of military rail traffic in operations, such a policy is justifiable.

In the absence of modern railway signalling military railways used forms unheard of in civvy street. There were Line Clear Tickets, Caution and Special Caution Tickets and Orders.

Line Clear Tickets were white and were used in Telephone and Ticket working to authorise a train to travel normally through a section at 'Line Clear'.

Caution Tickets and Orders were used when it was necessary to warn a driver that he had to observe caution in a section in which there was no obstruction.

Special Caution Tickets and Orders were used where a driver had to enter a section in which there was an obstruction, or possible obstruction.

These forms were distinguishable by colour, i.e. Line Clear Tickets—white; Caution Tickets and Orders—orange; Special Caution Tickets and Special Caution Orders—red. When the forms were used as 'Orders' the words 'Ticket' and 'You are authorised to proceed' were deleted and they were then not an authority to occupy a section.

This seemed all very complicated to me at Longmoor and I hoped that difficulties would never arise to complicate matters further. However, when the time came to work with these forms, the system was more readily understood; not only did we adapt, we also improvised.

There was always a need on active service to produce something on the spur of the moment and there was usually inventive genius available to do this. When we were short of Caution Tickets and Orders (orange) in Italy some bright spark came up with the idea of altering the wording on the white Line Clear Tickets and dying them yellow, the nearest caution colour to orange. This was done by making up a solution using mepacrine tablets for a base. There was an abundance of these yellow anti-malaria pills which were issued every day to the men as a protection against the disease. If their effect on our insides was anything like the stain they made on paper then we must have been yellow to the core.

Although the LNER Company was represented at Longmoor by locomotives and rolling stock belonging to my former employer there were no big tender engines or, for that matter, small tender engines. Tank engines were more suited to the LMR and quite adequate for training personnel in railway operating work since steam locomotives are basically the same. I had been looking forward to seeing, and perhaps driving, the

LNER 04 2-8-0 locos.

In the First World War 61 of these engines served in France and in 1941 this figure was improved on when 92 04's went overseas. Apart from war service they were widely employed on the LNER system where they found a home when they became surplus after the cessation of hostilities in 1918. The 04 had a nice 'LNER' appearance although the open cab belied its pedigree and seemed to suggest that its design had been influenced by other, less considerate, railway companies. The LNER possessed over 300 class 04's which were remarkably sturdy locomotives built by the former Great Central Railway.

Just before Christmas 1942 an important new railway in the Middle East was completed when General Alexander drove in a commemorative silver spike at Nahr-el-Kebir, Syria. The new line linked Haifa in Palestine with Tripoli in Syria, and apart from the Haifa-Acre section, which was undertaken by the Palestine Railways Administration, it was built by Australian, New Zealand and South African military engineers. The difficult coastal section between Acre and Beirut entailed the construction of massive sea walls, the driving of tunnels through rock and the spanning of numerous rivers by 15 bridges. The job was done by three South African Basuto pioneers, and a South African survey company.

Along this frequently precipitous line ran trains hauled by some of the 92 LNER class 04 2-8-0 locomotives and these were driven by men trained at Longmoor. Willie Fleming from Haymarket Depot, Edinburgh was one of these drivers and when I met up with him in Italy he punctuated his story of this railway by pompously remarking, 'No, Charlie, you could never have stuck it.'

In order to avoid the perpetuation of the 04's boiler which worked at a pressure of 180 pounds, the LNER fitted one of these engines, No. 6595, with a new type of boiler, carrying a pressure of 225 pounds, that had been used for the class B1 4-6-0 mixed traffic locomotives. A further modification was also made by fitting the same cylinders that were employed on the class B1 engines, with the Walschaert valve gear and modernised steam distribution arrangements. This came to be known as class 01 which had therefore the same boiler, cylinders, motion and as many other details as possible interchangeable with the renowned class B1 engine.

Over the years more than 150 locomotives of various types actually worked at Longmoor, but only two or three spent their entire working lives there. The place was a great 'engine depository' in the build up to D-Day and American and British Austerity locomotives which had 'cut their teeth' on main line railways eventually came under military control in the vast storehouse that was Longmoor. Amongst these were the LMS class 8's 2-8-0 and like the WD Austerities with the same wheel arrangement they were destined to have a long life.

Longmoor is well remembered by the many people who were trained there and survived the war—and the peace. William Thomson of Dunlop, Ayrshire who was a signalman at Kilmarnock until his retirement, can recall some of his experiences with the Sappers. He came to the Royal Engineers by way of an RASC unit in Wales. This unit was also at Newbury where it was formed into the 1st Airborne Division with the addition of three battalions of paratroops. After training in gliders and parachutes the War Office decided that the railway operations in France leading up to Dunkirk had been a failure, and it was decided to reform some railway operating companies, so Mr. Thomson was duly posted to Longmoor.

After training he was appointed to the position of guard and worked trains from Liss to Longmoor and Bordon. One day the Chief Royal Engineer (CRE) General Stone decided to visit Longmoor on a tour of inspection and one can well imagine the preparations for such a visit. The 0-6-2 tank engine 'Sir John French' was well polished for the occasion as also was the SR eight wheel saloon popularly known as the 'glass coach'.

A white line was painted on the platform at Longmoor as guidance to the driver in stopping the train and here was positioned Brigadier H.A. Joly de Lotbiniere MC, Commandant of the Transportation Training Centre RE, ready to welcome the CRE.

Mr. Thomson was the guard on this VIP train and after arrival at Liss where the engine rounded the saloon the crew waited pensively for the arrival of the General. As so often happens in the Army the top brass turned out to be more congenial than some of the officers preparing to welcome him, and he surprised everyone by asking if he could drive the train to Longmoor. Of course, his request could hardly be refused, and the train departed from Liss with General Stone at the controls.

On arrival at Longmoor the 'learner' General allowed the train to overshoot the platform, well beyond the white line and instead of the General alighting from the 'glass coach' there was only his aide availble to receive the well rehearsed welcome, and he was far removed from the white line. After moments of confusion and consternation, the General stepped down from the footplate, and as Mr. Thomson watched from the seclusion of his guard's van he thought, as people often do on such occasions, 'If only such chaos could be filmed!'

Shortly afterwards Mr. Thomson's company was posted to Weston-on-Trent where I had trained as a stoker on a stationary engine. There was a transportation depot on the Melbourne Military Railway called Kings Newton where rails were stored along with sleepers and other permanent way materials. One day while shunting there with a driver called 'Paddy' Mr. Thomson was approached by a captain in charge of a bridge building company, who were erecting a rail bridge across the River Trent. They had completed three quarters of the bridge and were ready for the final launch to the pier on the far side.

Unfortunately, the bogies carrying the section to be placed were so weighed down that the wheels refused to budge so the captain asked 'Paddy' to give it a push with his engine. It was a USA 0-6-0 tank engine which weighed 46 tons and had the outside drive on the rear axle. This drive was sometimes difficult to control and did not always respond to the steam regulator as is usually the case. A driver could pull on the regulator without result then suddenly the build up of steam would cause the locomotive to shoot forward. This is what happened when Paddy took on the job of giving the bridge section an even, sustained push. It was more like a push from a battering ram and the bridge section moved forward like some giant missile and might have taken off completely had not the drag chains restrained it and brought it to rest on the distant pier, where it was intended to be. Beads of sweat stood out on Paddy's red face as the captain and his bridging squad were horror struck and speechless with amazement.

From the 'horrors' of Weston, Mr. Thomson went to the Middle East where at Suez he was with No. 4 Docks Group which consisted of 1005 and 1012 Docks Maintenance Companies and 1003 and 1008 Docks Operating Companies. At that time King Farouk of Egypt had tried to escape to Italy with his private yacht but a British Navy destroyer persuaded him to return. The luxury yacht was taken along the Suez Canal to Lake Timsah and remained there until the end of the war.

Towards the end of 1943 Farouk wanted to visit King Ibn Saud of Arabia and the War Office arranged for a destroyer to be put at his disposal, and a cargo boat for his retinue, plus six white racing camels as a present for King Ibn Saud. Farouk, on his teturn to Suez, had with him a present of six camels from his host. While unloading same one of the camels fell out of the sling and broke its neck. As a consequence of this happening the CO of the Suez area decided the people concerned should be punished for such negligence and the vehicle plates of 1003 Company RE were painted back with an upside down camel picked out in yellow. From then on when sappers congregated the taunting cry was, 'Who killed the camel?' and this more often than not led to a scrap, which acted as a safety valve for pent up and frustrated soldiers.

As an LNER man it is difficult to believe that an LMS man could become confused with LNER engines. This happened to Sapper P.R. Williams, who had been a locomotive fireman and a Territorial in pre-war days. He was in France in 1939 and came back via Dunkirk then went into the Commandos. In 1943 all ex-loco firemen in his unit were sent on special duties—blowing up railway tracks, etc., firing, driving and repairing locomotives as well as putting them out of action in the shortest possible time. But before they could embark on this particular type of work they had to be trained at Longmoor and learn the intricacies of railway operating. Consequently, Sapper Williams found himself 'learning' to fire a steam locomotive all over again.

Two trainees were told by their instructor to climb aboard an ex-LNER tank locomotive and pointing to Sapper Williams the instructor said, 'Right, you first, Sapper, on the shovel.' Williams did all the right things, as he thought, he checked the water level in the boiler and looked at the fire, too. Said Williams to himself, 'Bloody hell! What small doors on the LNER jobs.' He broke all the coal up to the size of a man's fist (good text book stuff this) and duly stoked the engine round the course of about five miles, pulling eight vans fully fitted. As he later declared, 'I worked like the devil breaking up lumps of coal and flashing them around the box just like the book says, but it was difficult with that letter box firedoor.' However, the instructor was pleased with the trainee's performance and told him to change over with the sapper who was driving.

The first thing this worthy did was to swing two big doors open and reveal fully the interior of the firebox. He then started shovelling on lumps of coal as big as himself and Sapper Williams stood there in a state of amazement. There were no such doors on LMS locomotives and the uninitiated Sapper had, in fact, been firing through the inspection door! This caused a laugh amongst his mates for some time to come and today in Worcestershire, Mr. Williams can still see the funny side of the situation.

There was a great deal of shift work associated with the Royal Engineers. I had known these irregular hours in civvy street and again at Weston, Cairnryan and Longmoor. In civilian life a mother or a wife, or the man himself, would make up a packed lunch, or a 'piece' as it is known in Scotland. In the Army it was the cooks who prepared these sandwiches and served early morning breakfast at the unearthly hour of four o'clock or thereabouts.

The man rostered for an early shift would append his name to a list in the cookhouse where Army Catering Corps (ACC) and/or Royal Engineer cooks would be employed on the various tasks of food preparation. These men had an early rise at the best of times but those catering for the shift workers were up and about at three o'clock. Apart from their aptitude to cuisine and their culinary skills some of them displayed surprising dexterity. Like the cook who had been a drummer in a well known dance band. He would assemble the pots and pans on the large stove and with two big metal spoons give a first class display of jazz drumming. Men in the breakfast queue and others at the tables would stop in their stride to admire the talent and enjoy the sound of this impromptu performance.

There were funny incidents, too, in the cookhouse and ex-Sapper S.J. Harrison, now living in Gloucester, told me a tale that seems so typical of those far off days. Like me, Mr. Harrison had been a square peg in a round hole. In civvy street he had been a motor body builder while in the Army he became a carriage and wagon repairer on the railway at Weston. He was in the 955 Railway Workshops Company and worked for a while on the Melbourne Military Railway assembling pre-fabricated goods wagons from the USA. These consisted of 20 ton covered and open wagons and 'warflats' which were used to convey tanks. After about three months of this the company moved to Doncaster where they were employed at the LNER works. But it was at Weston-on-Trent, the camp I knew so well, that Sapper Harrison had a good laugh.

As was common practice in the Army, cooks engaged in making up packed lunches used to melt the butter and spread it on the bread with a shaving brush. I do not know if this was in the interests of economy or convenience but it was easy going. However, a cook was engaged in this task while preparing haversack rations for the next day when he felt a tap on his shoulder and a voice from behind saying, 'And what are you doing, Sapper?' Without turning round the butter spreader replied, 'I'm riding a b----- bike!' (Although the disguised expletive here is deliberately misspelt to avoid possible embarrassment to the reader, ex-sappers and other earthly creatures will be familiar with the normal expression.) On turning round the sapper cook's mouth fell open as he recognised the well known features of the Commanding Officer. Fortunately for the sapper the CO could see the funny side of the situation and gently rebuked the impulsive cook telling him to be more careful in future.

Although Longmoor is mostly associated with military railway training the Fieldworks Training Wing at Weavers Down was also of some significance. As a sapper, one had to be more than a railwayman and fieldworks training introduced men to the more serious business of war. They learned how to build bridges and explode charges and experiment with explosives. The people living down Applepie Hill and at Greatham did not take kindly to the loud bangs during the night when windows were sometimes broken by the blast.

Great stretches of Weavers Down were levelled and converted into marshalling areas for railway locomotives and other rolling stock which were made up into sets and dispatched either by the Bordon to Bently route or on to the Southern Railway at Liss.

New camps sprung up at Woolmer, Bordon and Weavers Down and old huts due for demolition were made watertight and given a new lease of life. Here it was that hand picked sappers were trained for such raids as

Vaagvo in Norway, St. Nazaire and Dieppe. Assault courses were designed and constructed around the rough country on Weavers Down, including what was once the swimming pool. These courses were rigged with diabolical traps to explode at the least intrusion. They were so cleverly adapted that OCTU courses used them.

Longmoor was a vast dispersal centre for British and American WD locomotives and was not too far away from the Channel ports where many of them passed on their way to the Continent. Although I never participated in the work of shipping these steam giants I knew people who did.

From a Railway Workshop Company at Doncaster 12 men were sent to Southampton on detachment. When they arrived at Kings Cross it was realised the CSM in charge of the party had been left behind, so they had to wait four hours in London until the sergeant major arrived, before proceeding to Southampton.

This was just after the capture of Cherbourg in June 1944 and their job was to send to France a large number of WD locomotives. These were dispatched on the *Twickenham, Hampton* and *Shepperton* ferry boats.

The sappers had to split the engines and tenders for loading purposes, the Austerities being too heavy to pass over the ship's bridge as one unit. The British locomotives presented no problem, but the USA 2-8-0's proved quite difficult to handle. Some of the steam piping on the boiler had to be removed to make way for the crane slings. In order to remove one particular pipe a man had to crawl into a filthy smokebox and uncouple a union nut using a spanner and large hammer. The sappers became so dirty that their clothes had to be changed every day.

The front pony wheels on the USA locomotives were held by a single kingpin and when the first loco was slung in the air these wheels dropped out and disappeared in the dock with a loud splash. The GI's who were doing the loading were not unduly perturbed and they made a kind of clamp with large belts to guard against recurrence. Altogether about 300 locomotives were shipped at this time.

The pins which secured the tenders to the USA 2-8-0 locos were pushed upwards and held in place with a plate and four large bolts. These could only be removed by compressing the loco to the tender and, hopefully, the bolts would drop out. The Yanks had their own particular method of separating the engine and tender.

They would place about six 2-8-0's against a buffer stop and, using a USA 0-6-0 tank engine would go back about 50 yards then charge against the big tender engines with some force. This had the effect of compressing all the engines and tenders and with a number of loud plops the pins would drop out.

Everything produced in America is usually larger than elsewhere but these American Army steam locomotives had to be restricted in size because of working conditions in the theatre of war to which they were destined. The massive engines used in America were completely unsuited for Europe and the UK and would probably have sunk axle deep in sand on the atrocious railways in the Middle East; consequently, America produced the S160 which was sent abroad in large numbers under the Lease-Lend in 1943.

Although truly American in appearance with the letters USA Transportation Corps on the tender, air pump in front of smokebox and sand atop the boiler other dimensions compared favourably with home produced locomotives. These locomotives could be adapted to use either coal or oil, they were dual fitted with air and vacuum brakes and the gradual steam brake was also incorporated in the stopping equipment. The reversing lever was similar to a signal lever and operated in a quadrant bracket where it engaged with notches to control valve travel.

Although the vacuum and air brake valve handles were at body level to the seated driver he had to reach above the pull out steam regulator handle for the steam brake and all these fitments were on the right hand side of the cab in contrast to the usual left hand drives in this country.

Right handed shovelling came more naturally to most firemen and a battery of main stop cocks were, as is normal, above the faceplate but in contrast to British practice the steam pressure gauge was sensibly fixed at eye level near the middle of the faceplate in line with the fireman's eyes as he stoked the fire, as also was the air pressure gauge. The vacuum gauge was above eye level.

Instead of the usual two water gauge columns there was only one on the left hand side. Replacing the other gauge column there were three boiler water level test valves set diagonally at different levels. When open the discharge from these valves went into a trough and was piped to below the locomotive. If the fireman had doubt about the water level in the boiler he could check by means of the test valves. In a real emergency when nothing of this kind was available I learned that a white chalk mark on the boiler plate could indicate the water level. So long as there was water the chalk remained white but when the water went below that mark it became discoloured.

The firedoor was of the battleship type and at a convenient height for shovelling. Rocker bars were a novelty and there were injector overflow indicators in the cab which avoided the need for the fireman to lean out of the window to see if the injector was working properly. Another innovation not seen on British steam engines was the blowdown cock. This was operated by a rod on the fireman's side and at a convenient time and place this cock would be opened to allow boiler sludge and scale to be blasted from the side of the boiler under full working pressure. All steam control valves had wheel type handles with spokes radiating from the valve spindle to an outer ring of spines which allowed for air cooling. The solid type of control wheel on British engines could become very hot and burn the uncautious. Last, but not least, the whistle was operated by a rope hanging across the cab roof with convient knobs dangling at each side.

These Yankee Austerities were built in America by three companies, Baldwin, Lima and Amco to a design by Major J.W. Marsh of the USA Transportation Corps. Apart from other types, including larger Austerities for the Russian theatre of war, 2000 'S160's' were produced. With the cessation of hostilities a great number of these locos helped to fill a widespread need in Eastern Europe and remained there for many years. In 1977 one of the veterans, No. 5820, built in April 1945 by Amco, was purchased from the Polish State Railways and shipped to England via Hull then transported to Haworth where the Keighley and Worth Valley Railway make good use of it under the name of Big Jim.

The working of the steam locomotive was basically the same in every type but the design varied a great deal. Apart from the general appearance, the location and style of cab and face plate fittings were according to the designers particular requirements. The reverser, steam regulator, blower handle and firebox door were four items prone to this inconsistency. There was the labour saving steam reverser, the convenience of which was cancelled out by its susceptibility to failure and the need for steam in its operation. In contrast to this near automatic control of directional travel there was the muscle developing signal lever type and the rotating upright or horizontal screw reverser. Their location on the right or left side of the cab was dependent on the most convenient side for signal sighting but, usually British locomotives were left hand drives.

The fulcrum point of the steam regulator handle was in the middle of the faceplate lined up to the steam slide valve in the dome. Operating extensions, however, could be the NB pendulum type with across push and pull movements. Similar transverse types were incorporated in other engines but with a low hanging lever. There was also the dual fitted pull out Gresley design and the ratchet steam regulator handle on the American Austerities which were right hand drives.

The blower handle was usually under the control of the fireman and NB engines had it well tucked away on his side against the boiler in the corner of the cab. Some engines out with the NB system, LMS for instance, had the blower handle in the centre of the faceplate and it was on this type that an interesting experiment was carried out at Derby.

Trouble sometimes occurred when the fireman omitted to turn on the blower before the driver shut the regulator, resulting in a blow back. A scheme was tried so that when the regulator handle moved to the right in closing, a pin projecting from the end of an arm attached to the regulator handle engaged the teeth of a stared wheel behind the blower handle, thus opening the blower valve. The idea was turned down as being too complicated to maintain. Gresley seems to have solved the blow back problem by simply positioning the blower handle within reach of the driver allowing the 'maestro' to open the blower valve prior to closing the steam regulator. This meant the fireman had to cross the cab to operate the blower in other circumstances but it was no great effort and he could always ask his mate to do the job if need be.

Firedoors could be of the battleship type which were oval in shape with a flap in the middle. These doors swung on two hinges on the right hand side. Firing was done through the flap while the doors remained closed and secured by a catch with a short chain attached. On some engines there were outer doors which protected the enginemen from the intense heat thrown out. NB engines had ratchet type doors which were rounded and completely within the firebox. When stoking these engines the fireman, or his mate, had to operate the door. There were drop doors hinged at the bottom and covering a round aperture such as those on the Director class which had a sloping firegrate. The sliding doors incorporated in LMS and BR designs were controlled by a single handle coupled to suitable rods and could be adjusted to conditions, opened or closed and stages in between. Oil burning engines had firedoors which were bolted with a small swivel cover over an inspection hole. This was the means by which a long steel rod with burning waste was introduced for lighting up purposes.

When my training on the LMR finished towards the end of July 1943 I was transferred to 'J' Company at the same camp. This was a kind of holding company which found work for men awaiting posting to operational units. There was always work in the cookhouse and the soul destroying job of weeding the grass verges near the officers mess. Before the rot set in, however, there came a call for volunteers to form a painting squad—Meacher immediately took the prescribed one step forward.

A wee Scots sergeant who had been a professional painter in civvy street interviewed the volunteers there and then, and when he came to me he asked, 'What experience have you had with painting?' 'I used to help my father decorate the house, Sergeant,' I replied. 'You'll do!' he said and with those two words I became a painter. Arrangements were made for the squad to rendezvous at Weavers Down Naafi next morning at eight o'clock, not for a cup of tea and a wad but to paint the place. In fact, we were destined to paint all the Naafi's at Longmoor and there were four including the permanent pre-war buildings known as the 'Brick Naafi', close to what were tin RA barracks; there was also a YMCA.

Longmoor Downs Station: Wot! No seats! The British Army get down to it in a replay of the evacuation of Dunkirk. In view is former LSWR Class 12 0-4-2 Locomotive 625. War gave this engine a new lease of life and sappers dubbed her 'The Emerald Queen', a title most suited for the prestigious duties undertaken by this veteran.

Sappers in wartime garb with regulation haircuts learn all about railway construction by the best possible method—practical experience.

Longmoor Military Railway: Bordon 15.7.42. Locomotive WD 2401, formerly SR 2019, arrives at Bordon with two Warflats and a brakevan. This is where Canadian ATS girls hitched a lift on my train which later broke a coupling en route to Longmoor.

The author at Longmoor in 1943. Aged 23, I was designated Railway Engine Driver (RED) Steam.

Sappers contemplate the next move as they study the precarious position of 'Train Set No. 3' which appears to have burst the points (29.4.42). Locomotive No. 7362 (LNER) eventually went to No. 2 Military Port at Cairnryan from where it was scrapped.

Eight-wheeled saloon No. 111 in Hollywater Loop 29.6.42 hauled by LSWR Class 202 No. 213, the only one of its kind at Longmoor. This loco's army career ended with a crash in Toronto Sidings in November 1943 when the breakdown squad was alerted before the collision occurred.

More trouble on the LMR at Liss Forest Road, Locomotive No. 7056 (LNER) derailed on 29.4.42.

Time for a break in the Hollywater Loop where Class 01 1046 was used extensively for training engine crews. This ex-Southern Railway Loco was built in 1894 and lasted until 1948 when it was withdrawn by BR.

Marlborough ex LMS Class 0-6-2T looking immaculate with headlamp at chimney level. This 1909 veteran from the North Staffordshire Railway appeared to be in good order but was, in fact, mechanically unsound and unsuited for shunting duties. The driver, fireman and instructor on the ground were distinguishable by their blue overalls and engineman's caps, with chevrons to further sort them out. Note also the inevitable re-railing ramp beside sandbox.

No. 203 Sir John French takes on water at Longmoor. Note the insulation on the water column against frost, also the re-railing ramp behind headlamp. 'Sir John' had a long, successful life at Longmoor during and between WW1 and WW2. This locomotive had numerous fitments to facilitate the training of sappers in various types of equipment, including the Weir steam feed pump and outside Walschaerts valve gear.

Largs Bay, *Aberdeen and Commonwealth Line. Troopship Cardiff to North Africa via Greenock 1943 (author aboard). Emigrant ship to Australia post-war years. These ships were named after bays in Australia, the most notable being* Jervis Bay, *sunk in combat with U Boat while, as an auxiliary cruiser, protecting convoy HX84. As a result convoy was able to scatter.*

On 2nd October 1942, while serving as a troop ship, the Queen Mary *accidentally rammed and sank HMS* Curacoa.

USA Class 2-8-2. American Locomotive Co. (ALCo). Royal Engineer Sappers. Loco numbers ranged from 42400 to 42490—these engines on arrival from USA were numbered in order of erection with date of erection on locomotive cab.

Tehran Shed. WD Class 8F. Royal Engineer Sappers. Enginemen, boilersmith, fitters. Sapper in centre sitting (a boilersmith) used to serenade us in bothy at Falconara.

WD (Ex LMS) No. 70308 in Jaffa Works Yard, 1944, after overhaul. Major J. Bird and Capt. Llewellyn RE of 199 Railway Workshop Co. RE.

WD (USA) 2-8-2 on mixed train Haifa to Cairo 1943. At El Arish Station, Palestine Railways.

Whether temporary or permanent, military camps were referred to as 'lines'. In a tented encampment, for instance, one could be instructed to 'keep the lines clean', that is, avoid dropping waste paper, etc. There is a story about the sapper who was seen wandering round the lines picking up discarded paper and cigarette cartons and examining this waste very closely. This went on for months until authority decided he was somewhat mentally disturbed and of no further use to the Corps. Consequently he was called before the CO and handed his discharge papers. 'That's it!' he cried. 'That's what I've been looking for for ages.'

The lines at Longmoor were sectionalised and had illustrious names including Ladysmith, Kimberley, Manton and Mafeking. Langley came very much later when Applepie had permanent structures built. There were Naafi's serving all these lines while the YMCA was known as Scymom Hall.

In the beginning I was very happy in the paint squad and we were never far from refreshments. Being excused all parades, only our surroundings reminded us we were still in the Army. There is something creative about painting and it feels good to be able to turn drab walls into colourful encasements using a suitable shade of paint to provide warmth and comfort. All this seemed very worthwhile but as the weeks went by I began to get restless, as I had been on occasions in the past when I wanted a change. This came in the most unexpected way and was an affront to my honour, but, on reflection, I daresay I deserved it.

We had reached our biggest and final task having started to paint the 'Brick Naafi'. Scaffolding was erected to allow us to reach the ceiling and frieze. It was the conventional wooden supports with an intervening plank and I sat on this structure plastering the high wall with distemper, as was used in those days. My position was high but my spirit that day was low—very low, and fed up, I started to slap on the colour holding the brush with two hands. Just then the sergeant walked in and called me down to where he stood at the door. 'Meacher,' he said, 'anyone who uses two hands on a paint brush is no good to me, report back to your company.' I had been sacked for the first time in my life and had, unthinkingly, brought it on myself. I was shattered.

The thought of going back to unskilled fatigues did not appeal to me, so for a few days I hung about the camp taking Naafi breaks, dodging the Regimental Police and occasionally going for a ride on the train. Very soon the strain of dodging became too much to bear and I went on parade with J Company again. Some unknown power must have told me to get back into line because on that first post-painting parade my name was called out. No mention was made of my abscondance so it seems the sergeant's advice to J Company regarding my severance from the paint squad coincided with my return to the fold.

For some time after I was more restless than ever until sent to nearby Woolmer camp where I realised the truth inherent in the adage, 'the grass is always greener on the other side'. But there was no grass at Woolmer, only mud and nissen huts. It seemed the place had been specially designed to demoralise men to the extent that they would gladly go anywhere to get away from its drudgery. In comparison Longmoor was paradise, limited as it was in recreational facilities, something of which Woolmer was completely deprived.

Soon after settling in my new abode I felt like an inmate in a labour camp. With indecent haste I was detailed with others to construct pathways and Woolmer certainly needed them. While engaged in this task one day cold rain fell to wash away the hot sweat on our brows, and we wore groundsheets. During a break in the downpour when the sun peeped through the clouds to warm our hearts I carried on working with my groundsheet round my shoulders. It was then I first met the most inflated sergeant major I have ever set eyes on. His obesity matched the rotund dimensions of a baby elephant and he spoke with a deep, Irish brogue. 'Who the hell do you think you are?' he said. 'Gladys Cooper? Get the b----- drapes off and swing that pick!' Looking up at this massive hulk I could see his battledress had been tailored for size and he wore First World War medal ribbons. There was obviously a soldier behind the facade and the smile on his lips was indicative of the man having a heart. After the introductory reprimand Paddy went on to praise our efforts and soon disappeared from the scene.

Although not unlike the squalor that was Flanders, the camp at Woolmer turned out a very smart and efficient guard. Men who were detailed for this military precision were drilled for five days and the result was quite commendable. To encourage smartness the best turned out soldier was given a day pass to London while the second best earned the 'stick', not a thrashing by any means, this was the name given to the man who took over the duties of messenger, a more relaxed job than sentry. In all there was an NCO and eight sappers and my turn soon came round to pound that parade ground for nearly a week. At the end of this time all the rust surrounding my soldier image had been removed and I felt ready to grace the pavement outside Buckingham Palace, never mind the entrance to Woolmer camp. After my last day's drilling, on the way back from the mess hut following tea, I stopped to read some notices. Soon I became aware of someone's mighty presence and I was dwarfed by the bulk of Sergeant Major Paddy. 'I see you're on guard tomorrow,' he mused. 'That's right, s'jin major,' I said. 'I'm just raring to go.' Leaning down to near the level of my left ear he whispered, 'Away you go and polish up your gear and I'll see you tomorrow morning.'

That evening I sat on my bed and worked like a trojan cleaning brasses and blancoing, I also ran short of spittal as I rubbed hard at the toecaps of my gleaming boots. Nor did I forget to polish the studs and clean the insteps—it was that kind of guard. Next morning at grey dawn, when Scotch mist hung low over that moorland setting I emerged from my Nissen hut before the camp was awake. Silently, the men I had marched with all week came from various locations to congregate on the road in front of the company office and there I joined them. There too, was the orderly officer and the unmistakable form of Sergeant Major Paddy. As I contemplated 12 hours of guard duty my sad thoughts were disturbed by the order to 'fall in'.

Even in the grey light we looked remarkably smart and I remember thinking, 'This lot is worthy of an audience—and a band, too!' But there were no ceremonies at Woolmer apart from the brief formality of mounting guard and that was seen only by the few participating. After falling in we were brought to attention and dressed off the marker. Then we had to call out as we numbered from the right and I was number seven. This was followed by 'Open order, march!' which gave the inspecting officer room to manoeuvre between the ranks. As I stood there rigid under the critical eyes of the officer and the sergeant major I felt confident I would be doing sentry duties. With hard work I had aimed for the ultimate but I would happily settle for the 'stick'. As these thoughts turned over in my mind the 'inspectors' were behind me and a touch on my left calf told me to raise my foot, like some horse being shod. Sure enough the soles of my boots were being looked at but they were as clean as the tops. In dusty places like India soldiers used to be carried onto the parade ground, piggy-back style by their servants and I was mindful of this when faced with Woolmer's mud. The two old rags I had wrapped round my boots now lay discarded in the waste bin and my boots were spotless. Then followed rifle inspection and the ignominy I had experienced with the rusty bayonet at Eastbourne was but a skeleton in the cupboard and cast no shadow over the gleaming bore of my short Lee Enfield rifle. The 'four by two' used to clean it the previous night had been pulled through umpteen times and the spiralled grooves which assisted the bullet on its way harboured a film of oil that protected the barrel's internal shine. The bolt, too, moved easily, smeared with the same special oil.

It was too dark to properly inspect rifles in the traditional manner, a thumb in the breach to reflect light into the barrel, while the inspecting officer peered down the other end. However, we all went through the motions and with rifles again at the 'port' position there followed the commands, 'Slooop-arms!' 'Close orderrr—march!' 'Righhht-dress!' This was closely followed by 'Number seven, right turn—dismiss,' called out in a most precise manner. It was music to my ears and I made straight for the company office where I collected a day pass and a ticket for London. Paddy had just seen the guard off on its way to change over and when I emerged from the office he smiled demurely and I have since wondered if I really earned my reward, which is highly likely, or was it some kind of affection Paddy had for 'Gladys Cooper'? After all, in his position he was not without influence.

As autumn changed to winter the rigours of Woolmer were even more severe and I became desperate for a move. Every Monday evening there was a 'request hour' when sappers were at liberty to see an officer and talk 'man to man' about anything or everything. This is the gent I went to see regularly about a posting. He soon got to know me and the stage was reached whereby he would see me coming through the door and call out, 'Nothing yet, Meacher!' Then one evening, late in November, as I made my entrance he cried in obvious delight, 'Ah, Meacher, I've got a posting for you—you're going overseas!' It was not quite what I had hoped for but as I gazed round at the misery that was Woolmer I realised the place had served its purpose, if what I believed was true. It had made me glad to go anywhere, even overseas.

The next few days saw intense activity in the camp. There were medical parades—innoculations and vaccinations—and the elderly Scots MO who did the necessary always seemed to be 'under a cloud'. I got the impression he had a close affinity with Scotland's national drink. When I returned to his Nissen hut clinic to let him examine my vaccination for effectiveness I knew that it had not taken. Not wanting to go through all that again I showed him the one I had done at birth. He was seated behind his desk when I put my arm in front of his face and as he lurched back somewhat unsteadily he gurgled, 'Lovely job—lovely job—next!'

Two of Paddy's incessant questions to the men became catch phrases and were always good for a laugh. These were, 'Have you all got your boots studded?' and 'Have you drawn your tropical kit?' I was not alone in being posted, there were many more joining the draft destined for nobody knew where. Our final parade at Woolmer was in darkness and Paddy stood on a high platform to address us in the light of lanterns. There was no doubt his wishes for us were sincere as he laboured to speak those stumbling words. His vast audience was hushed and I swallowed hard as I struggled in a sea of sentiment. Paddy could not have gone on much longer and his last faltering words came as a relief and were the cue for wild cheering. 'Good luck, lads,' he said. 'I wish I was coming with you.' There were cries of 'What!—and sink the bl---- boat!' and many more rude comments but it was a good way out of an otherwise sad parting.

We left Woolmer that cold, dark morning as a long column of shuffling humanity weighed down with all the paraphernalia allotted to a soldier.

There was an escort in the rear with red lamp to protect us, plenty of loud talking but nothing to sing about. The uppermost thought in our minds was, 'Where are we going?' but like the BO advertisement even our best friends would not tell us—it remained a well kept secret.

At Woolmer station there was a special train and as we sped westwards, dawn crept through the sky shedding pale light on sodden fields, a sight as dejected and miserable as many of us felt. At Swindon there was a change of engines and we left the crowded compartments to stretch our legs. We were not crowded as persons but engulfed by rifles and kit. Once on the move again we became aware of a roominess that had not been there before. The luggage racks were still crammed but two seats opposite me were vacant, the occupants having absconded at Swindon, leaving their kit behind. Because of lax roll calls their absence was not discovered until our arrival at our destination. But where was our destination?

Our approach to Cardiff only told us we were going on a boat. As the train passed very slowly on its way to the docks letters of farewell were handed to railway workers for posting. In this way the contents escaped the eagle eye of the censor and friends and relatives got to know that their soldier boys were sailing from Cardiff. Naturally I wanted Dorothy to know where I was but I was naive and when I sent a letter through the Army post office there was included a PS, 'Please remember me to Mrs. Jones.' The idea was for my wife to associate this with her friend in Wales, but I had not bargained for the alertness of the censor. He used his scissors on the PS and since I had written on both sides of the paper he cut away half the letter!

At Cardiff docks we assembled in a big warehouse in the shadow of the converted merchant ship *Largs Bay*, which was destined to be our home for longer than we expected—much longer. This ship survived the war and for many years ferried emigrants to Australia. In the warehouse there was a roll call of a kind but anyone could have answered to a name without the officer knowing. We were a mixed bag of reinforcements and there was no proper control until we were settled in particular units.

The *Largs Bay* cast off about six o'clock in the evening and before long we emerged from the Bristol Channel into the more turbulent Irish Sea. There was the novelty of buying any amount of chocolate and other things in short supply in Britain, but novelties wear off and soon we were contending with cramped messing and sleeping quarters (hammocks) and the Ancient Mariner's mournful cry, 'Water, water, everywhere' became more meaningful. For three days and three nights the Celtic Channel proved hard going for the old *Largs Bay* and harder still for soldiers who made poor sailors. Their vomit was everywhere and on one occasion the officer in charge of boat drill could not control his sickness and the ejection from his stomach simply gushed out and was carried clear by a strong wind. The only time I felt a bit squeamish was one night as I settled down in my hammock rocked by the thumping of the boat's engines. This nausea was stemmed by blissful sleep and I awoke early next morning and joined a few others up on deck.

It was the dawn of our fourth day at sea and quite suddenly we could discern the outline of some land mass. Was this our destination, we wondered, would the natives be friendly? We were certainly all at sea in more ways than one. We still knew nothing of the Army's plans for us. It was soon obvious by the closing distance between ship and land that we were leaving the open sea. The land mass grew ever bigger and I could see hills and isolated crofts just like my native Scotland. I soon realised it *was* my native Scotland; we were heading for anchorage at the 'Tail o' the Bank' near Greenock and there we remained for three days while I was tormented by local men bringing fresh water supplies aboard and the nearness of the tantalising hills of home. It was there in the Clyde estuary I saw the *Queen Mary* in battleship grey just in from America loaded to the gunnel with troops. Three days later we moved over to Belfast where we joined our convoy.

The speed of a wartime convoy is governed by the speed of the slowest ship and it seems the *Largs Bay*, formerly of the Aberdeen Commonwealth Line, was the governor. For a while we were entertained by British warships shepherding the sluggish convoy. It brings to mind the occasion, on 2nd October 1942, off the coast of Ireland, when the escort cruiser HMS *Curacao*, manoeuvring like a sheepdog, got in the way of the liner *Queen Mary* moving at high speed. On being struck with such fierce kinetic energy the cruiser was sliced in two. The Cunarder daren't stop because of the U-boat menace, and the Royal Navy sailors were left to founder along with their ship. There was great loss of life—over 350 dead and very few survivors. It wasn't long before our troopship was alone in the turbulent sea. No one could tell us where we were going and as I viewed the single Bofor gun near the bow of our ship my thoughts went to the sister ship *Jervis Bay*, named after a bay near Canberra in Australia.

This British armed merchant cruiser had been protecting Convoy HX84 in the Atlantic in November 1940 when the German pocket battleship *Admiral Scheer* came on the scene. The *Scheer*'s six 11 inch guns were too much for the *Jervis Bay*'s six inch guns although the British ship faced up to the superior fire-power and closed to within a mile of the German ship before being sunk. Captain Edward Fogarty Fegen, who went down with his ship, was posthumously awarded the VC.

94

His action allowed the convoy to scatter, although the *Admiral Scheer* chased them into the gathering darkness managing to sink five merchantmen out of 35. There is a plaque in East St. John, New Brunswick in memory of Captain Fogarty Fegen and the crew of *Jervis Bay* which was in the dockyard there before sailing into the Atlantic.

I had no desire to take part in similar heroics so I turned my mind to other things. The *Largs Bay* crew were very friendly and were either sworn to silence or ignorant of our destination. During the day our mess deck was spacious with tables to accommodate 12 persons but soon there were only three of us able to eat food at our table. We took it in turn to collect rations from the galley, always enough for the full complement. As we gorged ourselves, our sick companions were elsewhere wrenching their digestive systems and green-looking like the sea. I only felt sick for a few minutes one night as I lay in my hammock listening to the lullaby from the ship's engine—feeling the vibration, too.

At night complete darkness enveloped the ship and the sea, I was fascinated by the water's fluorescence and sometimes stood on deck watching this phenomenon. Sometimes there were cries of 'put that cigarette out!' Although warned of the need for total darkness there were people capable of risking the ship and many lives by indicating our presence to a marauding U-boat.

At night we had hammocks strung throughout the mess deck. To get to the toilet at this time one had to crawl under the suspended beds, bumping the occupants on the way. Some soldiers not cut out to be sailors slept blissfully on the mess tables, a more solid support for tired limbs.

Day after day, night after night the *Largs Bay* sailed on until, on the starboard side, we became aware of a profusion of lights reminiscent of Blackpool illuminations. It was all the more startling to people used to years of blackout. This was Morocco opposite Gibraltar, which was still in darkness. I learned that we had been going around in circles waiting for nightfall before passing through the Straight and into the Mediterranean Sea.

We were nearing the end of our long voyage and soon we were at rest in Oran (now Ouahran). The quayside was swarming with Yankee soldiers and vehicles. These courteous chaps helped us ashore with our baggage and guided us into the waiting trucks. One of our lads tripped on the gangplank under his heavy load and took a dive into the drink but was quickly rescued by an able American soldier.

In no time at all we were in convoy heading for Lion Mountain camp outside Oran. Our hosts were a US infantry company newly arrived from the States, they had never seen a 'Limey' soldier before and we were conscious of their great interest in us. The sappers wore khaki from head to foot but the tank corps men amongst us looked very smart with their black berets contrasting with khaki battledress.

The Yanks are great organisers, we were soon in the messroom being served food. Unlike the American divided mess tin the British 'dixie' as we called it was comprised of two separate metal dishes which engaged with each other when not in use. Our first meal was sausages and pineapple chunks washed down with tea 'especially for the Limeys' as one GI said to me. Rather than miss out on anything I took the sausages and pineapple chunks in one dish, tea in the other.

Later we were taken to our sleeping quarters, brand new cottage tents, new camp beds and only six men to a tent. What a contrast to the British Army bell tents, housing 18 men, feet to the pole.

As we settled in, a GI sat on his haunches near the tent flap viewing the British guys. What surprised him was our youthful appearance, so unlike the wrinkled, weather-beaten face of the average American soldier. Our visitor had been a taxi driver in Chicago and he amused us with his experiences of that Al Capone city. For a more vivid description of things he drew pictures in the sand with a stick.

I found these soldiers very friendly and helpful and in about two hours they had us fed and housed, and provided transport into Oran. I had half a bottle of Scotch whisky, a gift from my sister before leaving home. At a bar in Oran where French brandy was a popular drink I stood beside some GI's whose fondness for this brandy was beginning to ebb. As a sergeant drained his umpteenth thimbleful of the firewater I filled his glass with Scotch whisky. 'Gee!' said the sergeant, 'where did you get that, bud?' I just smiled and said 'Cheers,' and he continued, 'But why me? There are over 100,000 Yanks in Algeria and quite a few in this bar and you choose me to sample the best drink in the world—why me?' 'Well,' I said, 'it must be your lucky day!'

By this time the American soldiers were closing in on me as I held tight to my bottle of 'Scaatch'. The barmaids had stopped serving and with eyes wide and mouths agape stood in wonder at the sight of this rare drink. There wasn't enough to go round so we were soon back on cognac.

Later in the street on the way back to camp with my mates we came across an unusual military court. In an alcove an American army officer sat in judgement as dozens of GI's were brought before him by military police. Most of the offences were of a minor nature and were settled with a quick reproof and the offender released. More serious misbehaviour called for stronger action, the soldier being detained by the military police.

On 7th November 1942, late on, the largest amphibious invasion force the world had yet known assembled off the North African coast. More than 500 ships, ranging from converted cargo vessels to a once luxurious passenger liner had been used to carry 107,000 men and thousands of tons of weapons and supplies and landed them on the beaches of Morocco and Algeria. Little wonder the streets of Oran were crowded with GI's keeping the MP's busy.

Every morning the infantrymen were marched to the top of Lion Mountain in full combat kit and I used to sympathise with these weary soldiers on return. They were envious of the British Army boots and thought our forage-caps were 'mighty cute'. Pointing to his suede boots one GI said to me, 'This footwear is OK for walking down Broadway but no darn good for climbing that mountain.'

They were keen coin collectors, one of them offered me 10 dollars for a British threepenny piece. Too bad I had changed all my British money into French francs before leaving the *Largs Bay*. Jack-knives were another attraction to the Yanks especially those with a spike! I had lost my fountain pen on the way over so one day I went to the PX store, the equivalent of our Naafi. To the man behind the counter I said, 'I understand you guys are keen on jack-knives with a spike.' 'Sure,' he replied, 'have you got one?' I unhooked my knife from my trouser belt and showed it to the GI saying, 'I'll swap that for a fountain pen.' 'Sure, sure,' he said, 'don't go away,' and he went into a back room and brought out a fountain pen. 'Here,' he said, giving me a paper pad, 'try it out.' So I tested the pen, thanked him and handed over the jackknife. Looking back as I exited I saw the GI with the jack-knife held firmly, opening and shutting the spike, happy as a child at Christmas time.

On another occasion in the PX store I purchased the army paper 'Stars & Stripes'. For years I had had a 'foreign coin', a 10 cent piece with an Indian's head thereon, USA currency. I used it to purchase the newspaper and as I fingered the coin before parting with it the GI newsboy said, 'Great money, eh! You should get some more of it.'

One day the commanding officer at Lion Mountain camp ordered all British personnel on parade. I had visions of climbing the mountain along with the GI's but on reaching the parade ground we found a wooden platform had been erected and there was the CO on top with a tripod camera. When we were lined up he said, 'Hi, you guys, I want to take your picture for the folks back home, show them when I was in charge of the British Army.'

The Yanks certainly didn't need any reinforcements in Algeria, so what was the sappers' mission? Someone in Whitehall would have known but we didn't. Very soon we were on the move again and I found myself sharing a bivouac with another sapper in desert conditions near Algiers. Having been a steam engineman in civvy street I was interested in the railway in Algeria and visited Constantine and Philipville. Instead of open wagons full of coal as in Britain I was seeing much larger open wagons full of oranges.

Then came the time to move on and we boarded a ship at Algiers and ended up in Naples. This city in the shadow of Vesuvius had been badly savaged during the Allied advance on Italy and when we disembarked we actually walked across the side of a sunken ship to reach the quay. For a while we stayed in a tented transit camp on the slopes of Vesuvius, little knowing that this active volcano was due to erupt. Then we moved into Fascist barracks in Nola and I was put in charge of a few Italian POW's and given plans for the construction of latrines. The job was not unlike grave-digging and the Italians were fun to work with.

After digging a very deep and long hole, much bigger than a grave, they would attempt long jumps and usually ended up in the hole. When I remonstrated with them they would pull a long face as only an Italian can do and say, 'O, Carlo, lavore niente buono,' (work is no good). These men had been resettled and lived locally. More than once I was invited to their homes to partake of food and wine and violin music.

My real purpose of being in Italy soon followed. Along with other sappers I entrained at Naples and travelled to Taranto to join the 192 Railway Operating Company RE.

The 192 ROC RE was a mixed bag recruited from other Railway Operating Companies in Persia and the Middle East, also reinforcements from the UK, I being part of the latter induction. When I arrived at Taranto station there was a party of veteran sappers to meet us. To avoid humping my kit bag to the exit at the end of the coach I pushed it through a large drop-light (window) and cheerfully called on one of the reception party to assist. 'What do you think I am,' he said, 'a b----- porter!' That was my welcome to Taranto.

Some of these old hands (ex 193 ROC RE) proudly wore the Africa Star medal ribbon—too proudly, according to the envy shown by soldiers who had worked on the railway in Persia (Iran). These disappointed fellows comforted themselves with the rumour that Joe Stalin was having a special medal awarded to them for their excellent services in Russia.

These 'forgotten men' had operated the single line railway between Bandar Shahpur on the Persian Gulf via Tehran to Bander Shah on the Caspian Sea, taking much needed war equipment in the direction of the USSR. I used to listen to their tales in between songs in the canteen.

The 153 and 190 ROC RE arrived in Persia in 1941 and found a fairly well built railway 866 miles long which later had branch lines added. The locomotive stock imported from Europe was, on the whole, in poor condition like the wagons and passenger coaches that worked two goods trains and three passenger trains a day.

There was no opportunity afforded to learn roads and the language used was hand signs, the usual railway signals being similar to those in the UK. The Persian workers were very cooperative and train loadings were soon boosted.

The first WD Stanier 8F steam locomotive was operational before Christmas 1941 and other oil burners were turned out at regular short intervals after that.

Most of the British enginemen were young and inexperienced, but they were rudely acclimatised under the hot sun and through long smoke-filled tunnels skirting mountains 4000 feet above sea level on ruling gradients of one in 67. Torn Italy must have been cool in comparison according to a veteran who ended his dialogue with, 'Aye, Charlie, you could never have stuck it.' He also told me about two Americans in Persia who could not 'stick it'—they fell asleep on the job! The engine wheels then started to slip on the hot rails and as the grinding continued wheels and rails became one molten mass and welded together. This unusual metal 'sculpture' came to be preserved in the United States Army Transportation Corps museum.

The armistice with Italy was signed on 3rd September 1943 and it was the policy of the Allies to reinstate Italian railwaymen as quickly as possible. While repairs were being effected in the wake of the retreating German demolition squads British sappers waiting to man the trains were allocated duties of a supervisory nature over the Italian railwaymen.

While at Taranto I sat for weeks watching a signalman pulling levers on a hydraulic signalling system. Every time he pulled a lever there was a squelching noise from the operating plunger outside the door. I also travelled with Italian train guards (capo treno) and enginemen (mechanista and focesta) saying nothing, just making sure the wheels kept rolling between Taranto, Bari and Brindisi and towards Naples.

Later, I became RTO at Modugno near Bari (capo stazione) and catered for the wagon requirements at a local cement works and an RAF bomb dump at nearby Bittetto. There were also a succession of troop trains and endless wagon loads of armaments.

Civilian demands for rail travel like the requests from wine merchants for freight wagons had a very low priority. The occasional passenger train that was sanctioned was always filled beyond capacity with people and their luggage on the roof and the inevitable youths or men astride the rear coach buffers.

This was the kind of train that stalled in a tunnel at Salerno on 2nd March 1944 when 526 people died in tragic circumstances. The Italian steam locos on these trains were coal burners using inferior fuel that gave off dust and fumes. The dust caused a stinging sensation and the fumes had a choking effect. Add to this acute congestion on the train and the natural tendency for Latins to panic and you have the recipe for disaster in a confined space.

It was at Modugno I first saw a live German soldier.

Each day at dawn I had to check overnight arrivals in the goods yard. There was a wee office in the goods shed where the wagon checker's book was kept and as I entered this shed one morning I saw movement in a heap of straw. Thinking it was probably rats I carried on to the office and collected the book.

As I retraced my steps to the station sleeping quarters the heap of straw began to rise and I was confronted by two big Afrika Corps soldiers, dishevelled and bearded.

They didn't understand English and I was a stranger to the German tongue so we conversed in Italian.

It transpired that these two giants (who could have eaten me had they a mind to) had escaped from a prison camp near Taranto, boarded a goods train and alighted at Modugno, where I found them in the straw.

I took them to my sleeping quarters where a fellow sapper was still abed, opened the door and ushered them in ahead of me. When my sleepy mate saw the Germans he jumped up in bed, grabbed his rifle and tried to look aggressive.

'Alright Ernie,' I said from behind, 'go back to sleep, I'll make the breakfast.'

For a while I sat on my bed talking with the Afrika Corps men exchanging news and views, showing family photographs. Suddenly I realised it was time I told somebody about the incident.

We were attached to a nearby Stores Company for pay and food—not discipline—that came under our HQ at Bari. I phoned the Stores people and told them about the German POW's and in no time at all a sergeant and armed escort was at the door. The sergeant wore WWI medal ribbons and when he saw the Germans sitting on my bed he nearly had a fit.

Brusquely he ordered the enemy to get on their feet and quick march to the guardroom—'Left, right—left, right—left, right,' he shouted, English words the Germans responded to.

At Taranto I would stand on the footplate and watch the agitated mass of humanity struggling for a place on the train. One woman I saw looked remarkably well turned out in a sparkling white dress dazzling in the sunshine. When I looked closer I recognised the material as being terry-towelling, at that time on issue to the army. Another woman was wearing a heavy brown dress and barely discernable in the small of her back were the black letters 'US', the sign of an American army blanket.

These people certainly were resilient and adaptable and when it came to dressing for religious ceremonies a mosquito net suitably bleached and designed would not have looked out of place in the Vatican.

Taranto was a great Italian naval base where a swordfish from HMS *Illustrious* under the command of Andrew Browne Cunningham once flew under a harbour bridge in an attack on the Italian fleet. It was also the port of entry for Stanier 8F locos and American 2-8-2's transhipped from the Middle East. At Taranto, motions were reassembled and coal burners converted to oil burners in only a few days. The engines then went north to Fabriano and Falconara where I made their acquaintance.

Outwardly the oil burning steam engines were not unlike those that every little boy wanted to drive. It was when one climbed into the cab and took notice that differences were apparent.

In the tender compartment reserved for coal there was a suitably shaped tank for holding a large amount of crude oil, about 2000 gals. This was fed to under-slung pipes through a main stopcock to the front of the firebox where the oil burner was housed. Below this feed there was a steam atomizer both of which were controlled by the fireman in the cab.

The firebox of the 'Yankee Baldwin', as we called this type, had a foundation of firebricks surmounted by a brick wall on all sides, a kind of inverted brick oven, below a brick arch. The firedoor hole was covered by a heavy metal plate secured by bolts, with a small inspection cover on a swivel near the middle.

The converted Stanier 8F firebox had crossed brick beams as a base with brick walls and brick arch, the firedoor cover being similar to the Baldwin.

There had to be a supply of steam before the fire could be lit, either from the loco itself or from another source. There was an adapter at the side of the smokebox for this purpose.

A long steel rod was available for lighting purposes, the idea being to insert a lighted piece of cotton waste through the inspection cover in the hope that it would ignite the oil spray in the firebox. This was not always successful, so, very often, kindlers dispensed with the long rod and simply threw the flaming cotton waste into the firebox.

It was quite a simple matter on the American engines but the crossed brick beams on the British locos called for an accurate throw, otherwise the burning waste went down into the firepan and was doused.

Meanwhile, oil was dribbling from the burner on to the steam spray below and eventually into the firepan and the ground.

After about six attempts the frustrated fireman would be cursing as he manipulated the oil and steam control valves mindful that his efforts were creating a highly combustible substance. Then as the seventh flaming patch of waste entered the primed firebox there came a dull explosion shaking the loco to its wheels, followed by a thick smoke which quickly ignited as oxygen punctured its density.

As the flames raced to devour the oil deposit in the firepan and on the ground the engines became engulfed by fire. Momentarily, it was a frightening sight and Italian enginemen more used to 'carbone' (coal)

101

would flee panic-stricken. But soon the flames became confined to the firebox with only slight traces of smoke and blistered paintwork to tell of Vulcan's wrath.

The sappers in the army's railway operating companies were shy of provoking the 'God of Fire' although their impatience contributed to some extent to a dangerous situation. The main fault lay basically in the design of the converted '8F' firebox, there were fewer problems with the Baldwin engines originally designed as oil burners.

As an engine driver (trade category RED) with the 189 ROC RE I was based at Palombino, near Ancona and used to travel to the engine shed at Falconara, a former wagon repair shop which replaced the destroyed loco shed at Ancona.

There were Italian coal burning engines as well as the American and British oil burners. We worked shifts, and army discipline was relaxed as we laboured to make operational the railway the retreating Germans had so thoroughly sabotaged. Their demolition work destroyed bridges and rolling stock and lumps were blown out of alternate rails. Sometimes our adversaries would mount a large heavy hook, a scarifier (now in the Museum of Army Transport, Beverley, Humberside), onto a wagon hauled by several engines which went along the track tearing up sleepers.

Indian Railway Construction Companies did a great deal of repair work followed by maintenance. There were large gangs of them, their favourite meal being jappatti and sweet tea with plenty of milk. Sitting on their haunches the Indians' thoughts might have been of their homeland— their dress of loin cloth and sandals certainly was sub-continent.

Their chattering as a group sounded like the inharmonious jabbering from a flock of magpies or jays. Occasionally one, or maybe two Indians would leave the group and approach a locomotive saying, 'Water, Johnnie, water.' This was an indication that they wanted hot water to infuse with tea and sugar in a container, the dispenser being the locos steam water injector.

It is a simple matter to supply cold water by this means, but water at a high temperature often ejects with some force. This is what happened when I first tried to oblige two Indians, the tea and sugar mix was blasted out of the container and hot water splattered over the half naked railway soldiers from India. Their howls and loud Hindu obscenities alerted the others who laughed loud and long at the teamakers' predicament.

As they called up to me in English, 'Johnnie, Johnnie, Johnnie—no good Johnnie,' I offered to make amends and produced my own tea ration. On seeing this gesture big smiles came to the faces of the dark skinned duo. 'You have more, Johnnie?' asked one and I immediately thought, 'What a greedy b-----,' then I realised he was interested in doing a deal—he wanted to swap his beer ration for my tea and sugar which suits the Indian palate better.

My mate and I became good friends of the Indians and it transpired their beer came from Holyrood Brewery, Edinburgh while their battledresses were Canadian pattern. At that time our ration of beer was one can of Canadian 'White Horse' a week (poor quality) and our uniforms were Indian pattern, ill-fitting and impregnated with anti-gas powder.

We used to visit the Indian NCO's mess where I sang 'Indian Summer' and brought tears to the eyes of those homesick Hindus. They knew not and cared not at all that the song's sentiments referred to climatic conditions elsewhere than their homeland.

That seemed to be their attitude on another occasion when they removed a stretch of rail and went off to cook jappatties without leaving a warning sign. This resulted in a train of armoured tanks going over the embankment.

The oil burners were mostly used for mainline work on the Adriatic coast and were necessary because of the shortage of coal. Some Italian engines were coal burners but they represented work for the fireman and little comfort for him or the driver—there were no seats—the men stood on cement slabs.

These coal burners were preferred for short trips when there was a chance of trading the coal for fresh produce. But on the long trips north to Rimini or south-eastwards to Fabriano the oil burners—British or American—were the sappers' best friend.

Some skill was required to 'tune' an oil burner, the controls could be as sensitive as those on a radio. Combustion was near perfect when only a blue haze drifted from the chimney. Whereas a coal fire thrived on a strong draught up the chimney an oil jet required a soft consistent draught. The super-heater elements on oil fired locos were sometimes damaged by what was known as 'spot heat' caused by long periods of running with the steam shut off.

The oil jet could be tuned to burn like a handlamp or rage like a furnace. There was no ash deposit to impair coverage of the heating surface, the firebox was a chamber of intense aluminous flame, a swelling mass of oil vapour in a state of combustion. This was the ultimate desire on the mainline, hauling a heavy train, but in the shed the requirement was quite different.

To maintain steam and water during a standing period it was necessary to give an engine a 'blow up' every two hours or so. This meant the steam raiser would light the fire, providing sufficient oil feed to create the heat necessary to increase the steam pressure and fill the boiler. Once this had been accomplished the engine would stand fireless for another two hours or until it left the shed.

There were fitters and boilersmiths to attend to maintenance but there was no segregation of workers as was usual on other railways. We found a common identity as sappers of the Royal Engineers and shared the same conditions and amenities. On the night shift we would sit in the messroom-cum-bothy talking and joking. One sapper, a boilersmith, tended not to become involved in idle chatter and would sit staring into space softly singing popular songs of the day. His favourite song was 'I'll Be Seeing You' and as he went on about 'all the old familiar places' there was no doubt about where his thoughts lay.

The storage tanks on oil burning locomotives were replenished from a big tank propped up on brick supports. After removing the lid from the loco's tank the delivery pipe was inserted and the main delivery valve opened. The tank lids were secured by thumb-screws and it was important to ensure that these were tightly in place in order to prevent spillage caused by vibrations or derailment. Steam heating was provided in winter to maintain fluidity of the oil.

It can be very cold in Italy where snow and frost create the same problems encountered on British Railways. So it was that in the winter of 1944 the oil storage tank at Falconara failed to deliver, the valve was frozen. At least, that's what we were led to believe and we carried on working with what oil was available on the locos. Engines with empty tanks just stood waiting for the thaw.

This serious situation eventually came to the notice of the 'boss' Colonel Gardiner, who, as Brigadier, became Director of Transportation and Commandant at Longmoor in the post-war years 1948—50.

When he came to investigate the stoppage at Falconara there was a Stanier 8F standing with oil delivery bag in the tank and other engines waiting behind. The colonel immediately surveyed the situation as colonels do, then strode purposefully towards the wheel controlling the delivery valve. With one mighty heave he exerted great pressure on the stubborn valve and the wheel smoothly turned in the open position.

It was embarrassing for the sappers present who, guided by hearsay, had accepted that the valve was frozen. Perhaps it was ice-bound in the beginning and those people who had tried to turn the wheel were reluctant to exert too much force and cause serious damage to the equipment. Or it may have been that the winter sun climbing above the Adriatic directed its rays towards the colonel's effort! Whatever it was, it was an emphatic reminder of the army's teaching—'never anticipate' in other words never pre-conceive.

Driving steam engines in the army was not unlike the same job in civvy street. We worked shifts, wore blue overalls and had an affinity with steam and smoke and temperamental locomotives. In the war in Italy there was one significant difference, the driver and fireman each had a

Thompson sub-machine gun and we were trained to use it.

On taking duty the engineman would climb into the cab in the usual way with the gun slung over a shoulder. This was removed and hung up on the side of the cab ready for instant use. Only then did they set about stowing jackets and rations and preparing the loco for the road.

Sapper Tom Cormack (Dundee) and Sapper Harry Inett (Birmingham) had started the shift in the normal manner and preceded me on the road north to Rimini. I was still on shed with a Stanier 8F as they passed on the main line with their 'Yankee Baldwin' trailing a train of miscellaneous freight.

It was a beautiful night with a big moon casting golden splendour over a restless Adriatic sea. War and enmity seemed a million miles away and Falconara's red roofs glowed under a clear sky symbolising the peace that so many people craved. Only the train brought movement and soft sounds to the stillness of the night and very soon that was gone, leaving in its wake a tranquillity I was privileged to feel.

Tom and Harry did not get far that night, at Senigallia they collided with a Stanier Class 8F passing through a crossover tender first. Both engines were derailed and badly damaged and a dreaded fear was realised when the Baldwin caught fire.

No one was seriously injured and eventually the two locos were hauled back to Falconara. The Stanier 8F had a big dent in the back of the tender and the boiler of the Baldwin could not be recognised as such and lay crumpled in the cradle of the engine frame.

As I stood there viewing the sorrowful sight an old Italian engine driver sidled towards me and said, 'Inglese locomotive buona fabrica—Americano, no buona.' (The English locomotive is well made the American one no good.)

No doubt about it, the Stanier 8F was more robust but the mass-produced American loco was designed for a particular purpose and served this purpose admirably. The USA attitude to things mechanical nearing the limit of usefulness was 'scrap it and replace it' while the British sentiment was, perforce, 'keep it and repair it'. Consequently sappers on the east coast of Italy had to make do and mend while the more affluent Yanks on the west side had a seemingly endless supply of new replacement locos and parts.

Their locos also had superior water injectors and cab fittings, including armchair seats. The whistle cord and steam regulator handle came right into the driver's lap. The steam injector on the fireman's side was designed like a car handbrake. From a sitting position the fireman turned open the water valve and pulled up the steam handle and the injector 'sang like a lintie' as we used to say. The incidence of injector failure was less troublesome on Yankee engines. They also had test cocks to check boiler water level and in open country the fireman could pull a rod which released steam and water at high pressure from the side of the boiler thereby clearing scale and improving steam raising.

A classic example of improvisation I saw in Italy was when an Italian steam locomotive on a freight train had water leaking from its tank through a loose rivet. The tender also had a hot axle box. It was a case of killing two birds with one stone. The Italian driver fashioned a piece of tin to form a channel and secured this to the loose rivet so that the water was directed onto the hot axle box. This did the trick and the loco remained in traffic until it was due to return to the depot where proper repair facilities were available.

Many railway locomotives destined for a theatre of war were shipped as deck cargo and never reached their destination. Some were lost due to enemy action but many more went over the side in bad weather.

On shed duties one day at Falconara I was approached by an RASC corporal whose calm appeal belied the urgency of his mission. 'Could I have an engine sent into the oil depot quickly?' he asked. 'The place is on fire!'

The oil storage depot lay behind the improvised engine shed and there was stored the reservoir of oil needed to keep the 8th Army on the move in the relentless onslaught against the Germans. Apart from massive stocks of barrels oil was also piped from Ancona Docks and delivered by rail tanks. The latter was what caused great concern, there were 12 of these tanks brimful of high octane aviation fuel in the process of being discharged.

For obvious reasons steam engines were not allowed into the oil depot, diesel locos being used for rail movements. Ironically, there was no time to 'work to rule', I had to move fast. The nearest loco available was a Yankee Baldwin oil burner ready to leave the shed with an Italian crw.

'Presto!' I yelled. 'Andare deposito—olio cisternaas—Incendiamento! Incendiamento! Fire! Fire!' My call was a mixture of pidgin Italian and urgent English but the Italian driver cowered in the cab muttering, 'No buona, no buona.'

Impatiently, I climbed into the cab and took over the controls thus relieving the Italians in more ways than one as they made a hasty retreat.

The RASC corporal was there to pull points levers and admit me to the oil depot, where the approach was on a slight falling gradient. I was well aware of the need to be careful in introducing fire into an already incendious situation and screaming Italian civilian workers hurrying away from the blaze brought no comfort.

These people had been unloading barrels of oil from a road vehicle when one fell on its edge and exploded.

As I moved tender first towards the string of rail tanks I could see their ds opened wide, the sun reflecting on the clear fuel within. On the round nearby flames were racing along rivulets of petrol threatening the tacks of barrels on every side and large storage tanks on brick supports.

When the loco buffers gently kissed those of the leading rail tank the RASC man was quick to throw on the coupling and release wagon brakes. felt no fear, only a tingling excitement as I reversed the loco and applied and to the rail.

The 'Baldwin' had a ratchet type steam regulator handle which I pulled owards me and quickly closed again. This action was repeated in gentle elivery of the steam to the cylinders which I hoped would impart steady novement to the wheels. The desired effect was forthcoming as the riving wheels gripped the sanded rail.

There was only the reflection of fire from the engine as the Baldwin noved ever quicker away from the inferno. Looking back I could see the igh octane fuel swirling over the brim of the open tanks and streaming own the sides. It occurred to me we should have closed the lids before noving the tanks but just as quickly I excused this lapse with the thought hat time was not on our side.

Once underway I kept going until the dangerous cargo was well clear f the fire, rapidly spreading. The place burned for two days and mouldered long afterwards. We could see the plume of smoke from our illet in distant Palembino. Had those rail tanks not been moved so uickly the devastation delivered on Falconara would have ranked with he worst ravaging of the Italian peninsula.

The Zulus worked on the docks at Ancona and were encamped near Palembino. They were discouraged from drinking wine and other lcoholic drinks but one evening as I sunned myself outside my billet a ig Zulu sergeant with a big grin on his face and obviously a wee bit tipsy at down beside me. 'King George good, eh?' he grunted. 'Yes, yes,' I urriedly agreed. 'Doctor Livingstone good eh?' he continued, and went n to name other benefactors giving me a rib-crushing squeeze as I uickly responded with the right answer. It was a relief when he rose and taggered on his way to camp.

These proud warriors were told to go and sit in their tent when they did vrong and at football matches they used to entertain us at half-time lancing in grass skirts, holding spears.

There were no Royal Trains in Italy at the time but there were occasions vhen the Commander in Chief, Field Marshal Alexander, travelled by rain. On one occasion the 153 ROC RE had the honour of providing this ervice and the Chief himself took over the controls between Bari and San porito.

Unlike the American GIs whose overseas service was limited to 18 nonths the British squaddie had to soldier on until it was convenient to

107

grant home leave. However, there were compensations and with other tired sappers I spent a pleasant few days at Tricase on the heel of Italy, the 8th Army's rest camp.

More exciting was seven days leave while at Modugno, and I decided to tour Italy. I knew my brother, Jack was 'somewhere in Italy' with the 3rd Medium Regiment RA and I set out to find him. After a short train journey north from Bari I transferred to hitch-hiking by road. There was an abundance of army vehicles and lots of places to eat and sleep courtesy of the 8th Army, but my first lift in an army truck was on a big American Mack—huge, like all things American. En route I kept enquiring about the 3rd Medium Regiment RA until at a telegraph office in Pescara manned by South African soldiers I was told my brother's lot was attached to the 1st Canadian Division north of Rimini. When I reached this watering place I consulted a British military policeman, a red cap on traffic control. He was very helpful and confirmed that the Canadians were not far away. The next thing I knew the policeman had stopped a jeep occupied by a Canadian officer and driver. 'Give this bloke a lift,' he said—not a request but an order. I sat behind the Canadians as we bumped our way into open country and the dark. 'Where you heading for, soldier?' said the officer as he turned round in his seat. When I explained my business he said, 'You must be mad, leaving a safe haven for the war front.'

Eventually we reached a wooded area shrouded in darkness and I could see soldiers under the trees. As we went along the officer kept shouting to these groups of soldiers asking if the 3rd Med Regt was about. It was all to no avail and the officer said, 'You can stay with us for the night, then we'll look again in the morning.'

I was ushered into a big white villa near the sea, and down into a basement. There I found six big soldiers lounging and playing cards, all of them armed with revolvers. The CMP insignia on their shoulders told me they were policemen, the famous Mounties!

A former Glaswegian chatted with me and showed off some German souvenirs—war trophies. He told me I would be having dinner soon and so I waited and waited, until hunger tempted me to delve into my haversack for some iron rations. The ever watchful Mounties saw this and one said, 'We told you you'll be having dinner soon—put that away.'

Sure enough I was taken upstairs into a kitchen that would not have looked out of place in a five-star hotel. Cooks wore immaculate white dress and waiters passing to and fro wore blue military uniforms. I sat at a table as directed and watched this first class restaurant so close to the front line. Through the ever swinging door I could see officers dining off a white tableclothed spread—I was in the headquarters of General McNaughton, commander of the 1st Canadian Division, and shared his inner! Every course served to the officers was also served to me.

That night I slept in a comfortable bed attended to by the wee Glasgow chap, who turned out to be an officer's batman. Next morning, bright and early I had a good breakfast. My officer friend of the previous day came to see me and said my brother's outfit had gone to join the Poles in the central sector. He gave me a map showing the route taken and on reflection I remembered passing a convoy of gun carriers near Rimini. A jeep and driver was laid on to take me to the main road and my batman friend gave me a sandbag full of tins of British cigarettes—the Canadians preferred their Caporal brand.

Once deposited on the main road I started thumbing again and soon arrived at Falconara where the road to Jesi and central Italy branches off. I made a point of never thumbing ambulances for obvious reasons but as I walked towards Jesi an American ambulance stopped and a cheerful Yank called out, 'Where you going bud, want a lift?' Without waiting for an answer he was down opening the back doors and I found myself sitting awkwardly beside six bunks with six badly wounded Canadians occupying same. The driver told me as he slammed the doors shut he was going to Jesi hospital, 'but I'll drop you at the foot of the hill.'

I had been in this hospital with sandfly fever so I was no stranger to its location. After some hair-raising driving we passed my drop-off point and sped up the hill to the hospital. When the driver opened the doors and saw me sitting there he exclaimed in surprise, 'Gee, bud, I forgot all about you.' Being there, I helped with the stretchers before resuming my hitch-hiking.

In the main street in Jesi I came across a regiment of Scottish soldiers brewing tea at the side of the road, so I joined my compatriots for tea and blether.

My next stop was Perugia where I visited the British Military Police and asked about the 3rd Medium Regt RA. They told me my brother's convoy was parked near Assissi and offered me a bed for the night, but being so near I decided to carry on and find the gunners.

It was dark when I came across the convoy at the side of the road and nearly jumped out of my skin when a loud voice shouted, 'Halt!—Who goes there?' It was the sentry minding the sleeping soldiers. When I introduced myself and asked about my brother the sentry told me some men were bedded down in a nearby byre, others were in their trucks sleeping. I went to the byre and opposite a row of restless cows there were men under blankets sleeping on the floor. I went along this row of bodies uncovering each face and braving the stale smell of sweat, vino and cow dung. Unable to find Jack I reported back to the sentry who suggested I bed down in a mobile laundry and continue my search in the morning. I felt I could sleep anywhere so the dirty washing proved inviting.

Next morning I was up early and saw some soldiers brewing tea on a petrol fire in a field, a normal practice on active service. When I joined them for a brew I learned Jack was bedded in his truck and I hurried to the convoy. As I neared these vehicles the BSM was banging on roofs and shouting 'Wakey, wakey.' I asked him where I could find Bombadier Meacher and he gave a truck an extra hard bang and said, 'In here!'

I stood on a low embankment waiting for Jack to appear, then side curtains on the truck were raised and I saw two arms pushing aside gun parts followed by my brother's head. The look on his face was a mixture of surprise, emotion and sheer disbelief. Had he been static with a fixed address my appearance 'out of the blue' would have been astonishing enough but to find him while on the move in a foreign country was indeed surprise, surprise!

We were together two days, this RE joined the RA for meals and I slept in Jack's truck. In Assissi one evening we went to an ENSA show and were entertained by Issy Bonn and the Southern Sisters, newly flown out from England.

Time was not on my side, my short leave would soon expire so I said goodbye to Jack and headed for Rome, this time in an Italian farmer's lorry. On reaching this open and Holy city I went to the YMCA for food and lodging. My boots were covered in mud and when I put these before a wee Italian shoe shine boy his dark complexion changed to white. Bravely, he scraped and polished my boots and I rewarded him with a worthwhile tip to bring brightness to his face again.

Next day I was obliged to the American army for transport to Naples and to Foggia. From there to Bari the Royal Navy came to the rescue with a blue transit van. I walked into my 'bed sitter' at Modugno station at 2345. I had travelled more than 1000 miles, and my leave expired at 2359!

On 3rd May 1945 the German forces surrendered, the war in Italy was over, the 'D day dodgers' could relax. But there was still a British military involvement in Italy's railways. Many of the million defeated Germans had to be housed pending their repatriation and a great number of them were brought south by rail to a camp near Palambino manned by the Indian army.

There were soldiers, sailors and airmen, (some of Polish and Russian origin) recruited into the German ranks. We had a situation whereby American and British Poles were dealing with native Poles serving in the German army.

It was at Palembino I saw the proverbial 'mad Russian'. After the main body of prisoners had detrained and been spat on and abused by their former Italian allies, arrangements were made to transfer the lone Russian to a road vehicle. It took six British guards to control this wild man but eventually he was carried into a covered lorry and rushed away.

110

I don't know where.

These POW trains were made up of freight vans, some with an elevated rake caboose where the British armed guards kept watch. The Germans ere accommodated 12 men to each vehicle, with a bucket for toilet cilities.

Ventilation came from a small aperture near the roof and prisoners took in turn to stand on the bucket and view the scenery while at the same me filling their lungs with fresh air; the stench in those vans was verbearing after hours of confinement.

Cigarettes were hard to come by and gold watches and other precious ossessions changed hands for a single cigarette.

After my war effort at Falconara I was sent to Bologna engine shed, not work but to share an Allied presence with the Americans whose locos ominated the scene.

I liked their design of watering facilities at Bologna where a single large iameter pipe straddled the shed roads with a flexible hose serving each ad and giving local control of the water at tender height.

After a few weeks of envying the Americans their affluence and njoying their hospitality I went to Verona where I was housed in an partment block. Here on one of the walls I saw scratched the name of ount Ciano, the disgraced son-in-law of Benito Mussolini. I was told he ad been a prisoner in that building before his final exit from the scene. hese once illustrious people seemed to have a delight in graffiti. I saw ie name Field Marshal Albert Kesselring on the Bell Tower in Bologna. f course, there is no evidence that these people actually defaced walls, iey had their supporters to do it for them.

On 28th April 1945 Mussolini was killed by partisans along with his iistress Clara Petacci and a Fascist follower. They were strung up by the gs outside a garage in Milan where local people further violated the odies in giving vent to their wrath. This grisly display was hotographed and as picture postcards came to be on sale to the public long with the usual local views.

In Italy all German forces had surrendered but elsewhere there were ill pockets of resistance. It was not until 7th May 1945 that we knew for ire the war was over and this was confirmed when Churchill and ruman decided 8th May should be celebrated as Victory in Europe (VE) ay.

My thoughts had long dwelt on home leave and the leave train that ran om the south of Italy with connections from the Middle East to the hannel ports. The railway through France and Germany wasn't quite ady for this so the train went via Domodossola through Switzerland nd into France. There was a charge for this according to the number of xles passing over Swiss territory. Messing facilities were arranged at strategic points outside Switzerland, the first stop being Domodossola.

My turn came in November 1945 and the thought of seeing my wife and infant son after two years' separation was an exciting prospect. This took my mind off the discomfort on the train, the wooden seats, six men to a compartment and a mountain of kit bags.

The feeding areas en route were well organised and dealt with this huge influx of men very quickly. Announcements over the tannoy as soon as we stopped avoided any hesitation and delay, it was like a conveyor belt system, steady but sure.

In Switzerland the sparkling lights of neutrality were an added bonus and once through the long Alpine tunnels we made a brief stop at Berne, where we were greeted by crowds of Swiss people handing out chocolate and cigarettes, a tumultuous welcome, quite unexpected.

The French scene was more sombre but bright enough when we boarded the ferry at Calais for the short crossing to Dover. After an uneventful journey to London and on to Haworth in Yorkshire I eventually reached nearby Stanbury where my wife, Dorothy had acquired a small cottage, our first matrimonial home.

As we met and held each other close I experienced agitation of the mind, an excited feeling of pleasure, the old magic we had known but briefly during our short marriage. Then I said, 'Where is he?' and a smiling Dorothy went upstairs and returned with Brian, our first born, who I remembered as a six months old baby in white shawl. When Dorothy returned she held our son in her arms, a big boy in a warm dressing gown; she proudly presented him to me, now two and a half years old.

I spent a happy 28 days with them and it was nearly Christmas when my leave expired. Sometimes servicemen and women on leave at this time were told to extend it over the Christmas period to ease the pressure on transport. We were hopeful of receiving a telegram to this effect but this never came, and sadly I packed up my troubles in my old kit bag and returned to Italy, with a stop at a transit hotel in Folkestone.

By this time there was heavy snow in Switzerland and I remember the speeding train braking hard, sparks from the wheels reflecting in the snow, a winter wonderland it seemed.

My Christmas was spent in Verona where our unit was located at that time. I went to a concert there and ended up singing with an Italian orchestra the once popular song 'Goodnight Vienna'. Just as it was in Eastbourne when I sang with Gordon Rider and his band I had two violinists to accompany me—one on each side. But unlike Eastbourne the fiddlers accompanied me to the toilet and there continued to play as they encouraged me with, 'Encora, Carlo, encora!'—more! more! I was happy to oblige as it helped to stifle the hurt I felt at having to leave my wife nd son as they prepared for Christmas.

From Verona I went to Cervegnano where we lived in rail vans while
orking on the Friuli Military Railway named after that part of Italy.
This was in the disputed Trieste area which Italy and Yugoslavia argued
ver for years. It was also near Udine on the route to Villach and the
ustrian border. The engines on this railway were mostly Italian coal
urners.

Not far from our workplace was Gorizia, a city founded about the year
000 AD. The eastern suburbs are in Yugoslavia but at a placed called
The Castle' there is a massive monument overlooking the city and its
urroundings, rich in memories of the Battle of the Isongo during the
irst World War. It is reputed to be the largest war memorial in the world
nd this I can believe. The day I viewed this giant the massive stone
aircase disappeared into low lying clouds—like climbing up to heaven.

It was at Udine I said goodbye to military railways and war-torn Italy.
n 1946 I returned to the London and North Eastern Railway Company's
mployment at St. Margaret's depot in Edinburgh, a condition of my
elease when I volunteered to be a sapper.

There was no doubt here that locomotives burned coal, but by 1947
nis fuel became scarce and the LNER prepared to convert some locos
o oil burning. So convinced was management of the need for change that
alf a million pounds (a vast sum of money in 1947) was invested in an
il storage plant at Portobello.

Having had experience with oil burning steam engines I was asked
long with another ex-army driver to take on the job of instructor. This
readily agreed to but the coal crisis gradually faded, and heavy shovel
york with poor quality coal persisted for another 20 years until the
emise of steam on British Railways.

Now the oil burning steam engine is again coming into its own on
reservation railways where waste oil from garages has an advantage over
ostly coal. It all started when James Holden, Locomotive
uperintendent of the Great Eastern Railway from 1885 to 1907,
xperimented with oil burning apparatus on steam locomotives. The
rgency of Holden's experiments rested in the need to dispose of waste
mitting from a factory which made oil gas for lighting the Great Eastern
arriages. This discharge contaminated the rivers Lea and Channelsea,
o which the Stratford sanitary authorities objected most strongly.

Military railway sappers have Holden to thank for making their war
ffort that much easier.